For Douglas –

Rickshaws to Jets

A history a[nd ...]
of the Ke[nya ...]
1912-[1995]

Vera Harley

*Dedicated to my Kenya friends
in this world and the next*

*With love & best wishes
from
Great Auntie Vera Harley

Christmas 1995*

Published by Vera Harley
© YWCA 1995
ISBN: 0 952 6080 0 6

Rickshaws to Jets

Contents

Foreword iii
Acknowledgements iv
Abbreviations v
Author's Note vi
Map of Kenya vii
Preface viii

1. The Seed is Sown — 1912-1918 1
2. War to War — 1919-1939 23
3. Towards Integration — 1940-1954 46
4. Into the New Kenya — 1955-1965 58

Thirty Years On 149

Bibliography 151
Glossary 151
Nairobi changed road names 152

Front cover photograph: Dressmaking Class in Kikuyu. Mary Suthren top left.

Design and origination: Alan Slingsby
Printed by RAP, Rochdale

Foreword

The YWCA was the first organisation for women and girls in Kenya. As this history relates, for many years it served only Europeans but very early on, contact was made with World YWCA and letters suggest that the Association should consider opening its doors to all races. It took over forty years and two world wars before this came about. But there is no room nor reason for recrimination. Over those years a sound pattern of committee structure and voluntary service was being set up, money was being raised and hostels built, so that three years before Independence a true multi-racial YWCA was functioning in the country, comradeship and cooperation having been firmly established.

I have pleasure in writing this Foreword, and wish the Association in Kenya, and indeed all over the world, continued success in their important and challenging work.

[signature: Mw Kenyatta]

Miss Margaret Wambui Kenyatta

Acknowledgements

So many people have helped in putting this book together that it is difficult to know where to begin.

I am indebted to World YWCA in Geneva and to the YWCA of Kenya for granting me access to their archives. Marjorie Oludhe Macgoya supplied me with valuable information as did colleagues with whom I worked in Kenya. Peter Huth of Nairobi provided me with some very useful material. The recently retired National General Secretary of Great Britain, Elizabeth Sharples, spent a day with me in the Library of Warwick University going through the archives of the British Association. I invited myself to spend a week with an old friend, Pat Hodder, on her Somerset farm so that I could complete the first draft which she nobly and very efficiently checked.

Several friends who were with me in Kenya have been extremely encouraging and supportive; Elizabeth and Murray Normand, who gave me two and then three weeks hospitality in their house on the Isle of Mull, while working with me to commit the text to their word processor, Elizabeth subsequently doing most of the preparation of the text for the printer. Jean Whittaker, an old girl of Kenya High School, also helped considerably during this period, as did Mary Norton in sorting out the corrections on computer. Helen Haylett, Julie Williams and Pat Foley have all been of great assistance. Charles Richards gave me the benefit of his wide knowledge of East Africa.

Members of the C.M.S. staff have been very cooperative. Two friends who had known little about the YWCA or Kenya have, nevertheless, given valuable help; they are Valerie Porter who searched through records in London reference libraries, and Clare Clarke who helped me to coordinate the second draft.

Two TOC H friends must also be mentioned. Joyce Green who spent a day with me checking dates and facts, and Frank Rice who so ably edited the final draft and wrote the Preface.

To all these friends and many others whose names I have not room to mention, I am deeply grateful.

V. H.
London, May 1995

Abbreviations

A.G.H.S.	African Girls High School
A.I.M.	African Inland Mission
ASSOCIATION	Young Women's Christian Association
B.C.C.	British Council of Churches
B.F.D.	British Foreign Department, YWCA
C.&C.	Colonial and Commonwealth League of the Church of England Society
C.C.K.	Christian Council of Kenya
C.M.S.	Church Missionary Society
D.C.	District Commissioner
D.O.	District Officer
E.A.P.&L.	East Africa Power and Lighting Company
E.A.W.L.	East Africa Women's League
E&T	Education and Training
H.E.	His Excellency (the British Governor and President of Kenya)
I.M.C.	International Missionary Council
K.B.C.	Kenya Broadcasting Company
K.C.W.	Kenya Council of Women
M.M.S.	Methodist Missionary Society
N.G.S.	National General Secretary
O.F.D.	Overseas and Foreign Department (previously British YWCA Foreign Department)
P.C.E.A.	Presbyterian Church of East Africa
P.M.G.	Postmaster General
P.O.	Post Office
P.W.D.	Public Works Department
R.	rupee
S.A.C.S.	South African Colonial Society
S.O.S.B.W.	Society for the Overseas Settlement of British Women
T.T.C.	Teacher Training College
U.M.C.A.	Universities' Mission to Central Africa
VE Day	Victory in Europe — May 8, 1945
V.S.O.	Voluntary Service Overseas
V.T.S.	Vocational Training School
W.C.C.	World Council of Churches
W.R.N.S.	Women's Royal Naval Service
W.W.W.L.	Women's War Work League
YMCA	Young Men's Christian Association
YWCA	Young Women's Christian Association

Author's Note

The YWCA was founded in 1855 and World's YWCA in 1894; both began in London.

This book does not claim to be a full historical record, as there are gaps in the history which it has not been possible to fill. I have endeavoured, however, to include accounts of contemporary events in order to preserve the continuity, and to give the social and political background of this eventful period.

VH

National YWCAs mentioned
Australia
Bulgaria
Canada
Czechoslovakia
Ethiopia
Federal Republic of Germany
Great Britain
India
Japan
New Zealand
Palestine
Rhodesia/Zimbabwe
South Africa
Sierra Leone
Sweden
Tanzania
Uganda
USA

Associations in Great Britain mentioned
Birkenhead 1912
Liverpool 1912
Southport 1913
Alton 1915
Altrincham 1960

Any profits from this book will go to the YWCA
Further copies are available from:
YWCA Regional Office, 3rd Floor Central Club,
16 - 22 Great Russell Street, London WC1B 3LR.

"Each year God seems to press the needs of some portion of his great harvest field. This year the great Continent of Africa has been repeatedly brought to our notice... from Nairobi on the east, promising to become the Johannesburg of that part of Africa..."

Extract from A History of the World's YWCA
by Anna V. Rice,

from the Report of World's Executive Committee 1912

Preface

In this book, Vera Harley sets out to record and to explain the growth of the YWCA in one country — Kenya. It is an enthralling story. Moreover, her efforts have succeeded in setting out the story for us before records start to disappear and before the general memory has forgotten the immense changes that have overtaken this African country.

The latter part of the story came to life vividly for me because here the author was an active participant. This drove me back to the earlier chapters, based on written records, early minute books and some personal recollections of founder members, so that I could begin to understand how so few people could have achieved so much in such difficult times.

I welcome the chance to write this short, introductory note because I started to read the book knowing almost nothing of the YWCA — literally nothing of its growth and work overseas. I was fascinated to see in such detail how a handful of dedicated British and Kenyan women were able to build a lasting monument to real Christian service through a period of great political change and having to bridge huge cultural gaps.

This little book faithfully records their achievement and their heroic efforts deserve to be widely known and long remembered.

I urge you to read this book with all the care it warrants and then to ensure that all your friends read it too.

June, 1995 — F.G.R.
(Group Captain F G Rice, M.A., F.B.I.M. R.A.F. ret.)

The Seed is Sown
1912-1918

Nairobi, which means "sweet water" in the Maasai language, is situated almost on the equator at an altitude of 5,320 feet at the foot of the Kikuyu uplands, on what was a swampy plain through which the Nairobi River flowed. It is 320 miles from the old coastal town of Mombasa, which until 1907 was the seat of the British Protectorate Government.

In 1912 Nairobi would have been either dusty or muddy, for only the few main roads were made up and they were not tarred but of murram, a brick red hard drying earth. There were no pavements. The streets were lit by electricity as early as 1910 but for several years the supply was unreliable because the hydro-electric plant ceased to work during the dry season. The Year Book of 1912 describes Nairobi as a "busy town" and states that the Norfolk, Stanley and Carlton lounges were well patronised. It doesn't say that wild animals were still seen in Nairobi; one evening about this time a lion attacked the oxen pulling a private passenger wagon crossing Ainsworth Bridge. The railway station was very active, the line having been completed from Mombasa in 1899, and continued to Kisumu by 1903. Ox wagons waited at the the station for passengers off the trains. The Railway Institute was already built as were Garvey's Rooms in Government Road. These two buildings were used as theatres for the thriving amateur dramatic societies. In the Jubilee History of Nairobi we are told that there were two livery stables, one next door to the Norfolk Hotel, and the other at the house of Ali Khan in River Road. These stables supplied the animals to pull the mule carts, gigs and landaus which, together with the ox wagons and man-drawn rickshaws, constituted the transport. The local chemist was famous for his zebra-donkey cross which he harnessed to pull his private gig. A hitching post for animals was established outside the Standard Bank of South Africa in 6th Avenue. Cars were almost non-existent. Whiteaway's Building, the DC's Office, Nairobi House and the Nairobi Club were, by 1912, built and operating as was the Post Office in 6th Avenue which flew a blue flag when a mail ship had left Aden, a red one when the mail had reached Mombasa and a white one, (at night a white light) when mail was ready for distribution. Most of the buildings in the town were of wood, single-storeyed, built on stilts, with corrugated iron roofs. Some such buildings were still in use up to and indeed after Uhuru in 1963. The first Church in the town was St. Stephen's. Work on this timber-framed, corrugated iron building started in 1903. It was situated on the ground then occupied by the Church Missionary Society in Jackson Road.

Rickshaws to Jets

Although Nairobi is in the heart of the continent of Africa, there were few African women to be seen: they usually stayed on their shambas while their men folk ventured into the town to find domestic work in European homes.

There were, however, many Asian women — wives, sisters and daughters of the 4,350 Indians who had come to Africa to assist in the building of the Uganda Railway.

Young British women were arriving in ever increasing numbers, encouraged by the Colonial Office in London, to take up clerical and secretarial positions in Nairobi and Mombasa.

At that time there were only three countries on the Continent of Africa where the YWCA was functioning: Egypt (1876) South Africa (1886) and Nigeria (1906). Enquiries as to the possibility of setting up a YWCA in Nairobi first reached World's Office, in London, in 1911 and it was in that year that the YMCA opened their first building in Nairobi on the site where Brunners Hotel once stood and where Fedha Towers now stands. It was in the YMCA that fifteen British women met on what was probably a hot afternoon on Wednesday 14th February 1912, St. Valentine's Day, to discuss the formation of a YWCA branch in Nairobi. A Board of Management was formed and office-bearers elected. Below is a photostat of the minutes of the first meeting.

It is interesting to note the name of Mrs. Burns, a member of the original committee; she was an aunt of Gladys Beecher, nee Leakey, who many years later, became one of the first National Vice-Presidents.

These ladies certainly wasted no time, for according to the next minutes on 16th February, they met again. At this meeting they decided on a comprehensive programme of activities and also resolved that the Colonial Governor, Sir H. C. Belfield, K.C.M.G., should be asked to allocate a suitable site for the proposed YWCA building. The local press, the East African Standard and the weekly Leader,

The Seed is Sown — 1912

were to be approached regarding publicity about the formation of a YWCA and advertisements were to be inserted asking for premises which could be rented where the new Association could hold meetings. Readers were invited to give donations towards initial expenses. At this meeting a further resolution was passed that a letter be drafted to the British H.Q. in London asking what assistance could be expected in connection with the establishing of this new branch.

At the next meeting on 23rd February the question of Government assistance towards the proposed educational work of the Association was considered. It was decided however, not to make application for the grant-in-aid until the work had commenced.

On 28th February the Committee met yet again and Mrs Espie produced a plan of the top flat of Geater's building on the corner of 6th Avenue and Market Street, consisting of three rooms and a verandah. This was studied and it was decided that when Mr Geater returned to Nairobi in March, the YWCA should accept the rooms for one year at the agreed rental of Rupees 30 per month. A letter was read from the Government Secretariat acknowledging receipt of the Association's letter applying for land, simply saying that the matter would receive due consideration; there followed a discussion as to the location of a suitable site in Nairobi. Mrs Cruickshank, the Chairman, suggested that the neighbourhood of St Andrew's Church would be very acceptable, but there is no minute that a further letter be sent to the Secretariat at this juncture.

At this meeting a list of "practically all the young women and married ladies in the town likely to be interested" was submitted; this referred to Europeans only. All were to be invited to the YWCA's first social evening. Mrs Playfair referred to the question of admitting Eurasian girls but this minute reads "It was felt that in this matter the YWCA Committee should in the meantime follow the ruling of the YMCA but that later on, provision might be made for them." This history will reveal that it was to be over 40 years before any "provision" was made for non-Europeans. At this meeting the Hon. Treasurer announced that the first donation had been received, being Rs.75 from Mr Walter Graham of Magadi; this was only two weeks after the founding of the Branch.

By the meeting on the 11th March three more donations had been received, two of Rs.30 and one of Rs.20. The value of a Rupee was approximately Shs.1. 50. The Hon. Treasurer was instructed to open an account with the National Bank of India and to purchase stationery, rubber stamps, etc. This was an important meeting for the syllabus was drawn up: classes were to be available in Sewing, Cooking, Gardening, German, Swahili. Singing, First Aid, Painting and Bible Study.

The 2nd April was the last scheduled meeting for the President, Mrs Cruikshank, who was returning to England. The date of the first Social was brought forward to the 16th April so that she could attend. Final details regarding the programme and

The Y. W. C. A.

FIRST PUBLIC GATHERING.

The Committee of the newly-formed Nairobi Young Women's Christian Association held a social gathering in the Y. M. C. A. Hall on Tuesday evening and the proceedings were eminently successful. Numerous guests were admitted by the ladies of the Committee into a tastefully decorated room, which had been charmingly arranged for the occasion. There were about a dozen small tables, each surrounded by comfortable chairs, besides a number of seats disposed round the hall, and a delightful decorative scheme of flowers and greenery gladdened the eye. During the evening an excellent programme of music was provided and some good speeches were delivered.

The Right Rev. Bishop Peel presided, and the gathering was graced by the presence of Mrs. Bowring. Amongst those who sang were Mrs. Robertson, Miss Garvie, Miss Evans, Mr. Kendal, Mr. Alexander, and Mr. Evans, while Mrs. Espie accompanied.

At the outset, the Bishop of Mombasa having offered prayer, Mrs. McLellan Wilson, the Vice-President of the Society, in an interesting speech, explained the aims and objects of the movement, showing also that Mrs. Cruickshank, to whom they were with great regret bidding farewell, had been unanimously elected President. The next speech was by Bishop Peel, who said he had been asked by Mrs. Cruickshank to speak on her behalf and to mention the fact that she was too overcome at having to leave all her friends, and was thus unable to address them personally. The chairman then proceeded to show what excellent work was being performed by members of the movement all over the world, mentioning especially the branches at Bombay and Madras, with which he and his wife had been associated.

Mrs. Beaton, the Hony. Secretary, then spoke at some length on the practical work before the ladies in Nairobi, and announced that rooms had been secured in Sixth Avenue, namely the upper storey of Mr. Geater's building near the G. P. O. They would enter the rooms at the end of April, and furniture would be required to make them habitable, it being intended to provide a comfortable reading-room, class-rooms, etc. A series of classes would be arranged for the study of domestic and other subjects, and it was shown that the Association had no social distinctions and that its aims were high. She appealed to all the ladies present to become members and said that gifts in the shape of furniture and donations would be greatly acceptable.

The next speech was by the Rev. J. Youngson, who also backed up the movement, humorously referring to the success which the ladies were bound to achieve, and thanks were then accorded by the Rev. W. M. Falloon to Bishop Peel for presiding and to the young men for the use of their hall.

The singing of "God Save the King" terminated a very pleasant evening. During the proceedings a number of members were enrolled by Mrs. Dean, the Assistant Secretary, and light refreshments were dispensed.

refreshments were worked out and it was resolved that all ladies present at the Social be asked to become members of the Association, the annual subscription to be one Rupee. The Social Evening on the 16th April was obviously very successful as described in the press cutting (left).

The name of Mrs Radford of Mombasa is first mentioned on 2nd April. She had been invited to become a corresponding member and it was decided that she should be sent all information about the Association. As the only way young women from Britain could enter East Africa was through Mombasa, Mrs Radford promised to do everything possible to introduce all newcomers to the YWCA.

A special meeting had to be called on 16th April which Mrs Cruikshank was able to chair. A letter was read from the Secretary of the League of Mercy in which it was complained that an invitation to the YWCA "At Home" had been sent to a girl in the service of Mrs Davies of Jinja who had formerly been employed in the Nairobi Steam Laundry and whom the League of Mercy was anxious to keep away from Nairobi. It was decided that a letter be sent to the League assuring them that any girl invited by the YWCA to Nairobi for a special meeting would be received in a good home and well looked after while in town.

At Mrs Smallwood's suggestion it was decided to ask the Postmaster General if the P.O. girls would like to use the YWCA rooms during their lunchtime. She agreed to see the P.M.G. and report back. The meeting arranged for the 22nd April was cancelled "owing to the inclemency of the weather".

On 26th April a meeting was chaired by the Vice-President Mrs McLellan Wilson. An extract of a letter was read to the Committee from a Mrs

The Seed is Sown — 1912

Menzies editor of "Our Own Gazette" which was at that time the official newspaper of the British YWCA.

Mrs Menzies was also President of the Liverpool YWCA and she had written to Miss Picton-Warlaw, Head of the British YWCA Foreign Department asking her to do all she could to help the newly formed Branch in Nairobi. Mrs Menzies also mentioned having met a Miss Mather, who had worked for six and a half years with the YWCA in Barbados, and who was willing to work for the Nairobi Branch for £50 a year plus board and lodging, but nothing further is heard about her.

The next meeting on 30th April was the last one held at the YMCA. Mrs Smallwood was elected in place of Mrs Cruikshank. A sub-committee was set up to purchase the necessary furniture and equipment for the YWCA rooms. Mrs Espie and Mrs Beaton were elected to confer with the Land Office regarding a site for the YWCA. At this meeting a letter was read from the Assistant Corresponding Secretary of World's YWCA, Miss Ethel Knight, asking for details about the Association in Nairobi. It is interesting that contact should have been made by the World Movement when the Branch was only two months old. At that time World's H.Q. was next door to the British H.Q. in London.

On 8th May the Committee was able to meet in the Geater Building, the first YWCA premises in Nairobi. The scale of fees for membership and classes was fixed as follows:

Bible Classes	Free
One subject only	Rs.1
Three subjects	Rs.2.50
All subjects	Rs.5.00

Mrs Dean, one of the Honorary Secretaries, was asked to notify by postcard "all the Ladies who had intimated a desire to become members" about the dates of the classes.

It was resolved to write to Mr Curnow of the YMCA about the possibility of forming a joint YM/YW choir. At this meeting it was agreed that on Saturday nights there should be an informal social, the first of which should be on 18th May. The Chairman made several useful suggestions and offered to provide the tea and cakes. She also proposed that a leaflet be printed giving information about the work of the YWCA and that this should be posted to all European women in the Protectorate. Also a letter might be sent to one or more of the "Home", meaning British papers, "as it might catch the eye of people at "Home" interested in this country who might be disposed to assist"

At the meeting on 14th May, chaired by the President, it was reported that Mr Gosling, Postmaster General, had written offering to pay the YWCA Rs.15 per month for the use of their rooms in the Geater building by the G.P.O. female clerks during their lunch hour.

The two ladies who had been commissioned to see the Land Officer, Mr Barton-Wright, reported that they had found him very interested and sympathetic. He undertook to submit to the Acting Governor, Mr Bowring, a request for two acres in the vicinity of the Government School on which it was intended to build not only a YWCA hall but also residential quarters to accommodate the YWCA Secretary and 50 boarders. As a garden and tennis court were considered to be essential two acres could not be considered excessive.

The joint Hon. Secretaries were asked to write to the H.Q. of the Girls' Friendly Society and to the Travellers' Aid Society in London informing them of the new YWCA Branch in Nairobi. Mr. Curnow had agreed to the formation of a YM/YW choir. It was now felt that sub-committees should be set up comprising two Board members and two others to deal with each of the various activities and to report regularly to the Board which from now on would meet only once a month. At the next Board meeting on 27th May, hardly a month, a letter was read desiring to know if the terms offered with regard to the YWCA building site were acceptable, and the Hon. Secretary "was instructed gratefully to accept the offer".

The following sub-committees were then set up: Devotions, Education, Music, Social.

Mrs McLellan Wilson pointed out the necessity of the appointment of a Library Sub-Committee "...as it was essential that the literature provided for the use of members be carefully selected." The reception of members was discussed and it was agreed that the Social Sub-Committee should arrange for someone to be on duty at the rooms even on the nights when there were no classes. It was also agreed that there should be a Hostess at the Saturday night Socials "who would be given a free hand to conduct the evening as she thought proper."

Membership of the YMCA Tennis Club was offered to all YWCA members at Rs.5 per annum. This was gratefully accepted.

A letter was read to the Committee on 17th June from a Mrs Linton asking if it was not usual "for the YWCA Socials to close with prayer and praise", and that she would like this rule followed. "The subject of this letter was considered by the meeting and when put to the vote it was found that a difference of opinion existed and in the absence of any rules bearing on this matter it was resolved to refer the question to the H.Q. of the YWCA in London".

The first financial report was submitted by the Hon. Treasurer, Mrs Couper, showing a bank balance of Rs.826.53 The Hon. Treasurer and Mrs. Dean were instructed to effect an insurance on the furniture now belonging to the YWCA. As for the monthly reports from the sub-committees the only one presented was from the Devotional. The others were asked to hand to the Hon. Secretary a monthly written report of their work. Mrs. Espie reported having an interview with Mr. Barton-Wright of the Land Office who indicated that the most suitable

The Seed is Sown — 1912

site for the YWCA was on the face of the hill immediately above Kirk Road. Mrs Espie had told Mr. Barton-Wright, that although the Association was very grateful for the grant of one acre, it was considered that double that acreage would be required in the immediate future as tennis courts were considered to be essential. He therefore agreed to write to H.E. the Acting Governor recommending that a further acre be leased to the Association at a nominal rental. Mrs Anderson reported that the East African Standard had kindly offered to insert a weekly notice of the YWCA activities and it was agreed that weekly notes should also be sent to the "Leader."

Mrs. Espie was about to go on leave and she agreed to call at the YWCA H.Q. in London and ask for information regarding the work of the Association both at home and abroad.

The meeting on 15th July was chaired by Vice-President Mrs Burns. A letter was read from the Land Office stating that the Governor had agreed to grant the Association two acres on the hill above Kirk Road. A report from the Devotions Committee was received, but although the Education and Musical Committees had sent in reports these were too late for the meeting. The Social sub-committee had still not produced a report. It was decided to expand the educational work to include French and Shorthand, and the Hon. Secretary was instructed to order French text books from London to be purchased by the students; Rs.10 was voted for these. The caretaker at the Geater rooms was to be provided with a new khanzu and cap. A letter was read from a Mr Murdoch intimating that he was starting a dancing class and asking for the Committee's support. The meeting resolved that this proposal was "outside the sphere of the Association" and the Hon. Secretary was instructed to write to Mr Murdoch accordingly.

The only matter of importance minuted on 12th August was that a YWCA Prayer Union would meet on the 3rd Monday of each month at 4.30.

On 9th September two letters were read, one from Mrs. Espie about her visit to H.Q. in London and the other from Miss Clarissa Spencer, General Secretary of World's YWCA, both on the subject of whether Social Evenings should close with prayer. Both letters were discussed and it was resolved that, until a residential secretary was appointed, Hostesses at the weekly Socials could "close with prayer or with a hymn and prayer if they so desired". It was now decided to order copies of "Our Own Gazette" for sale to members. According to Julian Duguid's book "The Blue Triangle", this periodical at one time had the largest circulation of any magazine in Britain. Also an order was sent to London for regular copies of "The Tatler", "Strand Magazine", "Woman and Home" and "Girls' Own Paper" these to be placed in the YWCA Rooms. Mrs Smallwood said she would arrange a monthly meeting for members in her home and Mrs McGregor Ross offered to give a magic lantern lecture.

Rickshaws to Jets

The Committee met again on 14th October. It was noted that girls working in Nairobi were having great difficulty in finding accommodation. The Committee agreed, however, that until a lady superintendent was found, the YWCA could not help in this matter. The Hon. Treasurer's Report showed Rs.1110. 90 in the credit account and Rs.807 in the Building Fund. It was agreed that all future money be paid into the Building Fund, and that a concert should be organised in January to raise money. Mrs Munroe, Chairman of the Music Sub-Committee, agreed to arrange this. It was also decided that a Sale of Work should be held towards the end of 1913. Sir H. C. Belfield, K.C.M.G., was now Governor and it was resolved that Lady Belfield be invited to become Hon. President of the Association. At this meeting it was decided that once a month the Saturday Evening Social should be "thrown open to gentlemen friends of members, preferably on moonlight nights, and on those occasions there should be two hostesses".

A letter was sent to the Treasurer of World's YWCA on 29th October explaining how necessary it was for the YWCA to be able to offer a Home in Nairobi and suggesting that H.Q. should give financial support.

The President chaired the meeting on 11th November when it was reported that a Mrs Ross from Birkenhead YWCA had sent a gift of materials for the sale of work. The Hon. Sec. was asked to write thanking her. The Hon. President, Lady Belfield, had written expressing a wish to meet the Committee and see the YWCA Rooms.

On 9th December it was reported that Kiswahili classes were not well attended. A letter was read from the YMCA General Secretary inviting YWCA members to their Christmas dinner, and the President invited local members to her Christmas "At Home" on the 28th December.

The first meeting in 1913 took place on 13th January when a letter was received from Miss Ethel Knight of World's YWCA staff enclosing the accounts for badges, motto cards, hand books etc. which had been supplied to the Nairobi Branch. The Treasurer was authorised to remit payment of the same.

On 10th February fund raising and publicity were discussed and it was decided to hold working parties to prepare for the sale in October. £20 was voted with which to purchase goods from Whiteleys in London. Large sums, however, were required for the Building Fund so it was agreed that a letter should be sent to the British East African Association in London asking for their support. Publicity was essential and permission was sought and given for notice boards to be displayed in various prominent places in Nairobi including the railway station.

At the meeting on 10th March a letter was read from the Secretary of the Women's League of the Colonial & Continental Church of England Society, in which it was suggested that a lady appointed by the League might carry on the YWCA work in conjunction with that of the Society. "While appreciating the proposal, it was felt by all present that the work of the YWCA must be carried on on interdenominational lines". It seems almost certain, that the YMCA and the YWCA were the only Christian organisations in the world working ecumenically, this being written into their Constitutions. Many years later a committee of African members was faced with a similar offer and as we shall see, came to the same decision.

The South African Colonial Society had written asking if the YWCA would act as the Society's Representative in Nairobi; to this the Committee agreed. It was resolved to hold the first Annual General Meeting during the third week in April... "so as to have the benefit of a moonlight night"

Thus a new YWCA was born — a Branch of the British Association, Britain frequently being referred to as "Home". In an endeavour to set the social period of the time, the minutes have been quoted in some detail. The story continues using any minutes, reports and letters available.

On 12th May the Executive Committee met and another letter was read from Ethel Knight expressing her satisfaction at the progress of the Branch and asking for further information.

Ten days later a special meeting was called to consider an offer by the Bishop of Mombasa, the Rt. Rev. William George Peel, to place "Bishopsbourne" his Nairobi home, in 1st Ngong Avenue, at the disposal of the YWCA for a period of fifteen months at a nominal rent of Rs.10 per mensum. The accommodation was for "young white girls". The Committee unanimously agreed to accept this generous offer and the Hon. Secretary was instructed to write to the Bishop conveying their appreciation. She was also asked to write to the Superintendent of the YWCA Homes in Durban and Johannesburg with special reference to the "calling of gentlemen friends on residents".

SATURDAY, APRIL 26TH, 1913.

Y. W. C. A.

First Annual Meeting

The first annual members' business meeting of the Young Women's Christian Association was held on Tuesday afternoon last in the Y.M.C.A. building. In addition to a large number of members, the following gentlemen who were present took part in the meeting, namely: the Revd. W. M. Falloon, Revd. J. Youngson and the Revd. G. Burns. Mr. Curnow, Y.M.C.A. Secretary, took the chair by special request.

The Hon. Secretary, Mrs. Beaton, submitted a most interesting report in which the work accomplished by the Association during the past year was fully detailed. Briefly, the syllabus was divided under the following heads: devotional, educational, social and musical.

Several lectures on nursing, domestic hygiene, anthropology and biblical history were delivered by well-known lecturers among whom the following may be mentioned: Mrs. Brinck, Mrs. Gain, Mr. McGregor Ross, Dr. Birkett, Dr. Arthui, Miss Allen of Cambridge, Miss Buxton of London and Dr. Mary Hooper.

The French and the singing classes, under the superintendence of Mrs. Beaton and Miss Munro respectively, proved not only instructive but enjoyable to the members attending.

The Government very kindly granted the Association a plot of land in the vicinity of the European school for the purpose of a building comprising a hall, class rooms and bedroom accomodation for young women. This will fill a much felt want in Nairobi as young women at present find it extremely difficult to secure suitable accommodation. The Association, which now has a membership of 103, purpose holding a sale of work with the object of raising funds towards the erection of the building, and it is to be hoped the public generally will give this most worthy object the support it deserves.

The Hon. Treasurer's report shows that the work is receiving the practical support of the community. Hitherto the donations and subscriptions to the general and the building funds have been most gratifying, and the thanks of the Board of Management are due to the various subscribers; but, as a comparatively large sum is required to erect and furnish a suitable home, it is anticipated that several of the more wealthy settlers will guarantee the amount required to complete the building.

The following ladies were elected to the executive and Board of Management, namely:—

President: Mrs. Smallwood.
Vice-Presidents: Mrs. Burns.
    ,,   Mrs. Espie.
Hon. Treasurer: Mrs. Sweenie.
Hon. Secretary: Mrs. Beaton.

Committee:

Mrs. Curnow	Miss Witcomb
Mrs. C Anderson	Mrs. Birkett
Mrs. Sergeant	Mrs. Tarlton
Mrs. Watson	Mrs. Cearn
Miss Munro	Mrs. Newland
Mrs. Linton	

On 30th June a Miss Lind, who, apparently was recruited locally, was appointed Lady Superintendent for the Home which was to accommodate 10 residents and to be opened on the 15th July. The boarding rates were to be Rs.4 per day, Rs.25 per week. The Home was to be open to members of all denominations and attendance at prayers would not be compulsory. A Mr MacMillan promised a donation of Rs.1, 000 towards setting up the Home. This was indeed an important meeting, for the lease of the Kirk Road site was submitted to the Committee. It stated that the building erected on the plot must not cost less than £500. The lease was signed and a cheque for Rs.75 was sent to the Land Office. Fortunately the rooms in the Geater building had been re-let, thus relieving the YWCA of any further rent.

The following letter from Bishop Peel, dated 14th July, was received:
"Dear Mrs Smallwood,
As I heard that the YWCA Committee were in some perplexity regarding the carrying on of a home or hostel for the purpose of the Association, I venture to offer the use of my house for 18 months in the hope that such an arrangement would help to tide over difficulties. It is a great pleasure to me to know that you can adapt the house to the needs of the Association and I have therefore now the privilege of leaving Bishopsbourne in your hands as my present contribution to the needs of the YWCA in Nairobi.
May God add His full and enduring blessing to all the kind efforts of the Committee on behalf of the girls and young women in our rapidly increasing town.
With best wishes,
I am ever sincerely,
William George Mombasa"

Until 1964 the title "The Bishop of Mombasa" included all the Anglican Communion in Kenya.

The first mention of the Nairobi Branch in The British YWCA Foreign Department's Minutes occurs on the 25th July 1913 headed "Nairobi Appeal" when a letter was read from Mrs. J. H. Tritton, World's President, asking the Committee "...to earnestly consider the possibility of sending a Secretary to Nairobi, in view of the great need for work among the business girls there".

About the same time she, together with the Hon. Emily Kinnaird, wrote to the Nairobi Committee recommending that they should cooperate with South African Colonial Society; it will be remembered that the Committee at their March meeting had decided to do this.

The September meeting was held jointly with the League of Mercy, which was apparently the organisation assisting young women to emigrate to East Africa. Motor transport must by now have been operating in Nairobi, for at this meeting it was decided to write to the proprietors of various garages asking if they would be disposed to arrange for a motor service at a special rate for YWCA residents, a concession which apparently had been granted to nurses.

Fund raising was in full spate; the sale of work had been successful and the YM/YW choir had given "a delightful concert". Unfortunately minutes do not say how much money these events raised. "Our Own Gazette" was selling well and had made a profit of Rs.28 in the first year. It is obvious that London H.Q. was giving publicity to members in Great Britain about this new Branch in Africa, for in 1912 we read of a gift from Birkenhead and now a cheque for £25 arrived from a YWCA friend in Southport.

In November the B.F.D. agreed to take responsibility for the Nairobi Branch... "as far as they are able".

At the meeting of the Nairobi Board, in January 1914 a resolution reads "In order to promote and extend the influence of the Association throughout the Protectorate, Referees be appointed in various districts to act as correspondents in matters affecting the work of the YWCA." These ladies were to be sent the minutes and invited to attend monthly Board Meetings. Mrs Giles appears to have taken over from Mrs Radford in Mombasa; other places with referees were Nakuru, Naivasha, Lumbwa, Kericho, Kiambu, Kisumu, Machakos, Limuru, Fort Hall, Magadi, Thika and Uasin Gishu; no names were given.

A Visiting Sub-Committee was formed comprised of members who would be willing to call on all young women newly arrived in East Africa and also to visit any members who were ill or house-bound.

Classes were now in full swing at Bishopsbourne including Shorthand and Typing. A typewriter had been procured for practising. Fees were to be the same as in Government Schools — Shs.3 per term or Shs.1 per month. School children could attend all classes free.

In March a YWCA Employment Bureau was established for girls who had been sent to East Africa by the Colonization Society.

People locally were beginning to take a real interest: Mr Martin of the YMCA kindly tuned the piano; the Rev. Scuthers gave a complete set of Everyman's Encyclopaedia for the YWCA Library; Mr Radley of the Theatre Royal not only lent his theatre to the YWCA for a fundraising concert, which made a profit of Rs.120, but generously gave a donation of Rs.100.

Early in the year a Finance and Building Sub-Committee was set up, comprising seven men! Meanwhile the Board agreed that during the "wet season" ornamental trees should be planted on the building site.

In London the B.F.D. decided to fund-raise for the new Branch and "Nairobi Drawingroom Meetings" were organised. Ethel Knight considered that the need was so urgent, that these Meetings should not only be held in London and S. E. England, but also in the North and in Scotland. The Bishop of Mombasa was on furlough in England and he agreed to be the main speaker at a drawingroom in Wimbledon. By April, £242.4.0 was invested in London for the Nairobi Building Fund and £184.4.8 towards sending staff.

The YMCA was complaining about the YWCA mail being delivered to them. The Chairman said that she had twice been to see the Postmaster about this.

The YWCA was not the only organisation appealing for funds. A public meeting was held to discuss how money could be raised with which to build a permanent Anglican church.

But war clouds were gathering and war was declared between Britain and Germany on 4th August. Four days later, two British cruisers shelled Dar-es-Salaam, the capital of German East Africa. The war had indeed arrived, and it was realised in Nairobi that the railway, the Colony's lifeline, was perilously close to enemy territory at several points between Nairobi and Mombasa. The only military force in the Protectorate was a battalion of King's African Rifles and a company was speedily despatched to guard the most vulnerable areas of the track. A German raiding party did set out to destroy a strategic railway bridge, which doubtless they would have succeeded in doing had they not been using an inaccurate British map! They were captured and brought back, as prisoners of war, to Nairobi.

The YWCA suspended all social functions "for the time being". In spite of the war, however, the September Minutes record that the monthly magazines had arrived from London as usual.

The weekly local newspaper "The Leader" had apparently printed a 1914 YWCA calendar. The Editor now wrote advising the Association that the 1915 edition would be increased to Rs.1. 50. He offered, however, to advertise these calendars and place them for sale in "The Leader" office.

The year ended on an optimistic and exciting note for a letter from London H.Q. stated that a Miss Maude Saunders would be leaving England on 1st March 1915 travelling to Marseilles by train. On 4th March she would embark for Mombasa where her ship was due to arrive in April. She would then travel by rail to Nairobi to take up her position as Branch Secretary. This was the year that Mrs J. H. Tritton completed her second term as World's President and was replaced by the Hon. Mrs Montagu Waldegrave.

Early in 1915 Mrs. Smallwood was in London and met Miss Saunders, whom she considered to be "the very person to undertake the various problems facing the Association." During April Miss Saunders arrived, her terms of service as Branch Secretary and Hostel Warden being £120 per year, £70 of which was to be paid by Great Britain and £50 plus free Board and Lodging by the Nairobi Branch. In May a letter was read to the B.F.D. from Mrs. Espie, now President, Nairobi Branch, expressing her pleasure at Miss Saunders coming. The letter went on to say that

The Seed is Sown — 1915

building could not commence because of the war. A letter was also read from Bishop Peel thanking the B.F.D. for sending "someone of such high qualifications".

Saunders was a name already well known in World YWCA circles, for Maude's two sisters were both deeply involved in the work of the Association, Una as General Secretary of the National Dominion Council of Canada which had been founded in 1870, and Grace in Bulgaria, presumably laying foundations for a new Association; it is recorded that YWCA work began in Sofia in 1922.

At the April meeting, the Hon. Treasurer stated that a financial system was to be set up: all monies were to be paid direct into the Bank and the Secretary would use cheques for withdrawals.

Hostel rates were reviewed; the cubicles which the YWCA had built in Bishopsbourne would cost Rs.3 per day and single rooms Rs.4 per day. In order to advertise the Hostel five notice boards were erected around the town and Mr Smallwood's permission was asked for a larger one to be put up at the Railway Station.

From the minutes it seems that the Smallwoods were about to leave Nairobi for they state that another bookcase was purchased to house the many books donated by Mrs Smallwood for the YWCA Library. More books were donated by the Rev. W. M. Falloon. Mrs Barry, the Hon. Librarian was about to leave Nairobi so it was suggested that a Hostel Resident be asked to take over the post and that the library should be open one afternoon a week.

Mrs Langridge of Machakos wrote offering to give any YWCA residents a holiday in her house. This must have been greatly appreciated by the girls, all fresh from Britain, at a time when young ladies were certainly not able to stay in an hotel alone.

Board Members now felt that it was important that they become acquainted with the ten residents. It was therefore agreed that every Committee Member should invite residents to their homes. A letter was read from the World's YWCA asking for requests for praise and prayers to be included in the YM/YW Week of Prayer and World Fellowship leaflet. The Committee replied asking for prayers to be included for the Nairobi Branch and thanks to be given for the arrival of Miss Saunders.

A Mr and Mrs Hitchings invited a party of residents and their gentlemen friends for tennis at their home. By now a tea party was a regular feature at the YWCA between 4. and 6.30 every Wednesday. This was open to all members and their friends at 25 cents per guest.

A typewriter was dispatched from London for Miss Saunders which cost £25 including transport. London held a deposit account for the Nairobi Branch and this sum was deducted.

The July Minutes reported that the Visiting sub-Committee was functioning well.

Rickshaws to Jets

In August Miss Saunders arranged for a special audit of all YWCA books and a deficit of Rs.123 was recorded. At the Autumn sales the Secretary purchased a roll-top desk with English locks for Rs.125 and a carpet for the Residents' sitting-groom. When more linen was required she would write "home"; apparently this commodity was not available in East Africa.

Subscriptions were reported as being in arrears and postcards were sent to all defaulting members.

Miss Saunders told the Committee that she had spoken to the Governor about the quantity of rock on the site allocated to the YWCA and he had promised to instruct the P.W.D. to examine the rocks to determine whether they would be suitable for building material. Unfortunately this was found not to be so.

Two letters were read from the YMCA, one inviting members to a social evening, and the other apologising "for the very objectionable comic songs which had been sung". It does not say where or by whom!

YWCA members had been accused of sending white feathers to men working in Nairobi. Miss Saunders was to write denying this. The white feather was a symbol of cowardice during the first World War and was sent to men who had not joined the armed forces.

A letter was received from Mrs Bowring, wife of the Acting Governor, who was heading up the Women's War Work League asking for assistance. Miss Saunders said that she would be prepared to become the Organising Secretary if some help could be found for running the Hostel. One wonders what happened to Miss Lind;there is no mention of her since Miss Saunders' arrival. By October Mrs McCaskill had offered to become Honorary Housekeeper at the Hostel which was now full. She insisted on paying her own board and lodging; this she wished to be regarded as her war effort.

In September the B.F.D. wrote reminding Nairobi that they had agreed to pay £50 towards Maud Saunders' support. The Department also wrote to Miss Saunders, whose contract was for two years only, asking if she considered a replacement to be necessary when she went on leave.

Bible classes were now held for Hostel Residents, Committee Members, YWCA Members and friends. These were apparently organised by Miss Saunders. The Devotions Committee met with the YMCA to make arrangements for the Week of Prayer and World Fellowship. Later it was reported that the Bishop of Mombasa and the Bishop of Uganda had both participated in the joint Service.

A Sale of Work was a great success, stalls including "home made goods, fancy stall and fish pond". The event must have continued after dark for Mr Gosling lent hurricane lamps, presumably borrowed from the Post Office stores. The Sale raised Rs.770.

The Seed is Sown — 1916

A gift of £35 was received from Alton YWCA in Great Britain. This was to furnish a room in the new Hostel in memory of Catherine Crowley who had been a member of that Branch.

Because funds were so limited, plans for the new Hostel had to be severely modified. Finally it was decided that one large rectangular room should be built of stone, inside which two wooden folding doors would be installed to form a dining room, a common room and a rest room. There would be a staircase at the north end and a hallway by the front door where, no doubt, the Reception Desk was placed. Above, accommodation for eighteen residents would be provided by building wooden partitions to make single and double rooms and some bath rooms. A wooden verandah would be erected along the east front of the building. The reader will say "What about the kitchen?" It was common practice in those days to build a temporary structure for cooking. The original kitchen, therefore, was in all probability a lean-to, built against the south wall of the large room. Probably the present chimney was constructed for a wood-burning oven opening into the kitchen. Some of the cooking would no doubt have been done on kerosene stoves. The servants' quarters, too, would have been of a temporary type, built to the south of the kitchen. It is difficult to imagine the first Hostel with no sanitation. Refrigeration would probably have been of the charcoal-drip type and later by refrigerators run on kerosene.

In July a YWCA Reading Room was opened to the general public, so in spite of the war the Nairobi Branch appears to have been progressing well.

Two concerts were given by YWCA members to patients in what had become the Combined General Hospital and, during Christmas, Hostel residents assisted the W.W.W.L. in serving mid-day dinner to patients in the surgical ward. The Christmas Programme in the Hostel included a Fancy Dress Dinner on Christmas Evening. It was about this time that World's YWCA circulated a letter to all Associations regarding policy to "certain forms of amusement such as the dance and drama which are increasing in influence and popularity in nearly all communities". It goes on to suggest that the YWCA should "educate young people in taste and discrimination".

Reporting on her work with the W.W.W.L. Miss Saunders said that she had met many new people and this should benefit the YWCA. By January 1916, accommodation in Bishopsbourne was found to be insufficient, some residents having to sleep in Mrs Brooke's bungalow, returning to Bishopsbourne for their meals. It was suggested that the verandah be enclosed to make some more bed space. Sincere thanks were expressed to Mrs MacCaskill Honorary Housekeeper at Bishopsbourne, who was shortly leaving for India.

A rather disturbing letter from Mrs Espie was read to the B.F.D. Committee in February saying that there had been trouble between Miss Saunders and the Hon.

Treasurer, the latter having resigned. This was probably the result of the audit which had been carried out in August 1915.

Another letter arrived in London, this one from Maude Saunders, explaining that, because of the war, building costs had risen, making it impossible for work to start on the new Hostel. She also asked that her "status in Nairobi be defined". The Committee replied that she was sent out to be General Secretary, Nairobi Branch, and that there must be a capable Matron for the Hostel.

In February, Bishop Peel asked the YWCA to vacate Bishopsbourne in April instead of June, so, although the Building Fund was still insufficient, it was decided to accept Mr. Blower's tender of Rs.27,489 and ask that the building proceed until funds ran out.

During March, the B.F.D. wrote to Miss Saunders asking if, after her leave, which would be due in March 1917, she would agree to return for five years.

Very sadly, Bishop Peel died of typhoid fever on 5th April; Bishopsbourne was therefore still available to the YWCA.

On 10th April Lady Belfield "cut the first sod" on the building site, and in June she laid the Foundation Stone which reads: "This Stone was laid by Lady Belfield on 29th June 1916."

After taking tea, Lady Belfield was welcomed by Mr Hunter, Chairman of the Building Committee, and introduced to the architect. Following the votes of thanks, Miss Saunders gave a talk about the world-wide work of the YWCA.

In May the B.F.D. wrote stating that they wished Miss Saunders to remain as General Secretary and Hostel Superintendent. Miss Saunders agreed to this, pending the opening of the new building.

In order to take over the running of the Hostel, Miss Saunders resigned from the W.W.W.L. She assured the Committee that her four months with the League had greatly benefited the YWCA.

The telephone at Bishopsbourne had been rented by the League and as Miss Saunders was no longer their Secretary, the YWCA had to rent their first telephone. It is interesting to note that the Board now decided to change the time of their meetings from morning to 4.30 p.m. This was probably because members were doing war work during the day. By the 1950s the Board was again meeting at 10.30 a.m. only to be changed again to early evening after Independence so that African members, most of whom were working, might attend.

A letter was read at the April meeting from Mr Orr, Director of Education, saying that he was recommending a Government grant of Rs.321.50 to the YWCA education programme. Classes were going well in French, Shorthand and Typing and Book-Keeping. Miss Saunders stated "It is a matter of special regret that so few members support the Bible Classes especially as so few opportunities for Bible Study are available." She hoped that "...these studies, which were of such fundamental importance, would be strengthened and developed".

The Seed is Sown — 1916

At the B.F.D.'s May meeting it was reported that the Nairobi building had commenced and that the money, held on deposit in London, was required. The Minutes go on to say that the World's President, The Hon. Mrs. Montagu Waldegrave "kindly laid this request before World's Committee, as World's YWCA also had money on deposit for Nairobi". A letter was read from Miss Saunders saying that Miss Ethel Gem, at present working at the C.M.S. Hospital at Mengo, would be leaving her post in October and was willing to become Housekeeper, a position for which she was eminently suitable. She required £50 a year "all found". Could the B.F.D. help with her salary?. The reply was that they would consider giving something towards Miss Gem's first year. When this news reached Nairobi, the Committee decided to ask the British YWCA for £30, the Nairobi Branch agreeing to pay the Board and Lodging plus £20, thus making up her salary. Subsequently this was agreed.

The Committee thought that it was time that Hostel residents had representation on the Board and a Miss Hunmock was recommended: it was further agreed that the Post Office girls, who were apparently still using the YWCA, should also be represented, and two names were suggested. In August it was decided to invite Children's nurses to have tea at the YWCA on their afternoon off. No doubt all these nurses were European.

Maude Saunders' reply to the B.F.D. was read at their June meeting. She stated that it would be necessary for someone to be sent out to replace her during her furlough which she considered should be five clear months. She recommended that the term of service for East Africa should be two and a half to three years and she agreed to return for a second period of three years. At this meeting, the B.F.D. decided that the terms of service for East Africa should be three years, followed by a furlough of six months. They then passed a resolution which was sent to Nairobi… "That as the Hostel is small, Miss Saunders should remain as Superintendent of Hostel, and General Secretary Nairobi." To this Maude replied that once the new building was open, she would not be able to combine both jobs but she hoped Miss Gem would have arrived by then.

Mrs Espie, Nairobi President, visited London in June and no doubt had long discussions with the B.F.D. She was invited to attend a conference in Oxford for YWCA Committee Members.

Miss Saunders now wrote to the B.F.D. asking what arrangements could be made for Miss Gem's furlough which was overdue. Presumably, as she had resigned from the C.M.S. they were no longer responsible. The B.F.D. referred the matter to World's YWCA. The name B.F.D. was now changed to Overseas Foreign Department (O.F.D.)

Among Maude Saunders' many attributes must have been music as she now agreed to teach singing at the High School, and to charge Rs.60 per term, the money to be paid into YWCA funds.

At the August meeting, Miss Saunders reported that she had been approached by Capt. Lunn of the YMCA regarding their fortnightly socials with lectures. It seems that all they required from the YWCA were cakes! She said that YWCA members did not attend because the dates of the socials were never received in time for them to be advertised.

In September Miss Gem arrived to take over as Housekeeper at Bishopsbourne.

A letter was received in October from Archdeacon Hamshere asking for rent for Bishopsbourne from March, at Rs.75 per month. He warned that it might be necessary to give only one month's notice but gave assurance that the YWCA would be reimbursed for all improvements. Apparently, new latrines had been built at the cost of Rs.40. The Minutes record that the Building Fund was Rs.9,000 short.

The W.W.W.L. asked Miss Saunders to become their secretary again. As Miss Gem was proving to be very satisfactory Miss Saunders agreed to work part-time for the League on two mornings a week. She also accepted the post as Headmistress of the High School from January 1917 until Easter. Presumably, she took this step to relieve the YWCA of paying her salary for three months, knowing that the new building would certainly not be ready before Easter.

It was decided that, if Bishopsbourne had to be vacated before the new building was ready, the educational programme and Bible Studies would continue either in members' houses or at the YMCA. This must have been an extremely worrying time for the Committee, knowing that the new building was far from finished and that the C.M.S. might reclaim Bishopsbourne at any moment. After much heart searching it was decided that the number of residents must be run down and one can imagine how upsetting this must have been for everyone concerned.

In spite of all these uncertainties, kind offers of gifts were coming in. Mrs MacMillan generously donated Rs.1,000 towards the furnishing, with a further offer to provide twelve fully equipped beds and the Rev. Southern offered to pay for the furnishing of a room. During this period there were frequent references in the Minutes to war casualties, and repeated expressions of sympathy were sent to those who had lost members of their families.

At the December meeting Miss Gem's appointment was confirmed for two years to September 1918. She was obviously living up to her name, for Miss Saunders wrote to London about her in glowing terms.

The year ended on a dismal note as the Hostel was only half built and the money had run out. However there is a minute reminding the Committee that H.Q. London were holding £932.14.6 on deposit for Nairobi.

The Seed is Sown — 1917

A letter from London H.Q. was read at the January 1917 Board Meeting stating that Miss Saunders would be expected to pay her passage home herself; this would be refunded when she arrived in London.

At the February meeting of the O.F.D., a letter was read from Miss Saunders saying that until the new hostel was ready, her time was not fully occupied and telling them about her appointment as Headmistress of Nairobi High School for three months prior to her sailing for home. A quarter of her salary would be equally divided between Nairobi YWCA and the O.F.D. The committee replied that, as she appeared to have the consent of the Nairobi committee, they would agree to this. But they pointed out that she should have communicated with London before accepting the post.

For years the various missions had been endeavouring to cooperate more closely and the war gave them a unique ecumenical opportunity. The military authorities required porters to create a Carrier Corps and the churches agreed to be responsible for the recruitment. In 1917, 2,000 volunteers assembled at Kikuyu to form this Corps coming from various Christian backgrounds. This gave the missions the chance of working together in ensuring that these men were given welfare and pastoral care, and no doubt it was a means of spreading the Gospel. Good always comes out of evil.

By now the Anglican church had raised sufficient money with which to start building. On 3rd February 1917 the foundation stone was laid and All Saints Church, although still incomplete, was opened later in the year.

On the 14th March The East African Women's League was founded. This organisation proved to be of very valuable service to the community in Kenya and on several occasions worked closely with the YWCA.

A letter to the O.F.D. was received in April from Mrs Saunders in which she said that her daughter, Maude, could not get home for her long leave because of the war. The committee wrote to Maude querying this.

At the May meeting of the O.F.D. a request was read from the Nairobi Committee asking that Miss Saunders be given permission to continue as Headmistress until a passage home became available. Mrs. Waldegrave told the O.F.D. that Maude had been corresponding with World's Office, apparently by-passing the O.F.D. The World's President said that she would ensure that a letter would be sent to Miss Saunders reminding her that she should write direct to the O.F.D.

The Committee in London decided to write to Nairobi stressing that the Building Fund money must be used for a YWCA Hostel. Presumably they were concerned because Maude was at the High School and waiting to go on furlough, leaving Miss Gem, ex-C.M.S. in charge. As this history will reveal they need not have worried.

In June a letter was received in London from Miss Saunders reporting that she had had a happy and successful time at the High School but assuring the O.F.D. that she had given all the time necessary to YWCA work. She stated that the Building Fund was £300 short but that she had "...promises of any part of this sum not immediately raised". The war had delayed the building programme but it was imperative that Bishopsbourne be vacated as soon as possible.

The Nairobi Minutes do not say when the new building was likely to be finished. The move seemed to be imminent however, because a letter was sent to London asking for advice as to "suitable entertainment for YWCAs, and in April the Committee decided that the electric light in the new Hostel should be on meters. In any case Bishopsbourne had to be vacated by 26th June.

Energetic fund-raising events were still being organised; a Garden Fete was held in Parklands Sports Club, and a Concert which raised Rs.737. The YMCA were asked for the loan of their premises for a Whist Drive. They replied that as the Army would not permit card games and many soldiers frequented the YMCA, they could not allow the YWCA to hold a Whist Drive there.

At this time many ships were being sunk, for the minutes state that the "...mail from home is now infrequent". However the Mombasa Referee reported that in spite of the war, girls were still arriving, being met at Mombasa docks where they were told about the YWCA in Nairobi.

A Girl Guide Company had been set up in Nairobi and the YWCA offered them the use of the new Hostel, when open, for their H.Q.

In September a cable was received by the O.F.D. from Maude Saunders as follows: "Resigning from Secretaryship Christmas desirable arrange successor overlaps".

About the same time a letter dated in August arrived in London from Mrs. Pritchard, Acting President Nairobi Branch, reporting that they had moved into the new building and giving details of the programme work being carried out by the Branch. As this letter had been written before the cable was despatched, the Committee decided to take no action until a letter of confirmation had been received from Miss Saunders.

October came and there was still no letter from Maude Saunders but another from her mother. She said that the main reason for Maude's resignation was that a good deal of advance work was being deferred because of her imminent furlough. This work could be started if a new Secretary were sent out. The O.F.D. decided, however, that no new staff could be appointed at that time and sent a report to World's YWCA.

By November the O.F.D. had received a letter from Miss Saunders, in which she gave her reasons for resigning as follows:
a) Her Mother's health.

The Seed is Sown — 1917

The extension to the hostel built in 1919

b) As Miss Gem had now been four years in the tropics, her furlough must not be postponed.

c) It was important to get development work started now. She concluded by thanking the Overseas and Foreign Department and said she hoped to work with the YWCA on her return.

World's YWCA wrote expressing their regret at her resignation and stating that they hoped she would remain on the YWCA Committee in Nairobi until she left for home. A letter was also sent to the Nairobi Committee saying that it was not possible to send another Secretary at the present time, and stating that it was "sometimes possible to reach Nairobi via South Africa". One wonders if they were contemplating asking the YWCA in South Africa to send staff, although this is not mentioned. The O.F.D. committee apparently had a long discussion regarding the work in Nairobi and the question was raised "…as to whether another staff member should be sent to Nairobi until a Kenya National Association be formed". This indeed was premature; the word National was not used in Kenya until Uhuru in 1963. When, in 1958, a N.G.S. was appointed, her title was queried, many people considering that it should be Colony General Secretary. The name British East African Protectorate was adopted in 1896 and not changed to Kenya Colony until 1920. So both the words "National" and "Kenya" were anachronisms.

The London Committee however decided that as the new hostel was built and operating, it would be unwise to relinquish work with the Nairobi Branch.

At the same time the O.F.D., advised World's YWCA to "…carefully consider the position of affairs in Nairobi". This veiled criticism of a young and struggling branch seems very unfair. There was no reason to suspect that the Committee or members were the cause of Maude Saunders' resignation.

It is interesting to note that in October 1917, The Hon. Mrs Montagu Waldegrave, World's President, is minuted to have said to the Overseas and Foreign Committee "...as foreign work was part of the British, it ought to stand or fall by it". There can be little doubt that it was her influence which prompted World's YWCA to write to the O.F.D. in December of that year, stating that the "Extension Committee of World's YWCA would continue to maintain work in Nairobi, as it had been with them that the hostel work had originated".

Apparently the World's Presidents, first Mrs. Tritton who served her second term from 1910 to 1914 followed by Mrs. Waldegrave, attended all the meetings of the O.F.D., and both showed great interest in and sympathy towards the new Branch in Nairobi, urging that it should be given maximum support. It seems strange that World's Presidents should have become so personally involved but three points must be taken into consideration: the first five World's Presidents were members of the British Association: most of the work overseas had been instigated by Great Britain: until 1930 World's HQ was based in London and from 1897 to 1919 was actually next door to the British H.Q. in George Street, Hanover Square.

It is not possible to say exactly when the first building in Nairobi became inhabited; we can only hope that they were able to meet the C.M.S. deadline of 26th June. Mrs Pritchard's letter to the O.F.D. establishes the fact that a hostel on the present YWCA site, was operating by August 1917. The move was probably towards the end of June, very rushed and hectic with no time for an official opening.

As there is now a gap in the Nairobi Minutes until 1921 there is no way of finding out when Maude Saunders managed to secure a passage home: possibly not until the end of the war in November 1918. If this was in fact the case, at least it would have enabled her to assist Ethel Gem in setting up the new premises and working together with her for seventeen months.

From records at World's Headquarters, it is stated that in 1918 the Kenya Association became affiliated to the World Movement as a Corresponding Member; a letter from Miss Clarissa H. Spencer, World's General Secretary, was written to Nairobi Branch confirming this.

Two years after the death of the YWCA's good friend, Bishop Peel, the Rt. Rev. R. Heywood became Bishop of Mombasa and on 31st July 1918 it was he who dedicated the still incomplete church of All Saints, later to be extended to become the Cathedral. This was an important year for the churches because, following years of debate and discussion, an Alliance of Missions was formed which included the C.M.S., A.I.M., C.S.M., and U.M.M. Bishop Heywood became Chairman of the Advisory Council.

War to War
1919-1939

In 1919 Nairobi became a Municipal Council with corporate rights. The necessary legislation had been approved ten years previously but the 1914-18 war had delayed this being implemented. The town's population was still only 14,000.

Because of the gap in Nairobi Minutes and the fact that nothing is mentioned in the British Overseas and Foreign Department's Minutes, we can only assume that when Maude Saunders ultimately obtained a passage home, Ethel Gem took over and held the fort until late 1919 when she went on her very overdue furlough.

There is a note in World's YWCA files recording that an extension was being added to the Nairobi Hostel; this must have been when Miss Gem was in charge. No details are available but in all probability the addition to the north end was built, comprising the Reception area, a staff flat and accommodation for residents above.

In 1920 the British O.F.D. Committee set up a sub-committee for Africa and in March their minutes stated that Miss Gertrude Walker had sailed for Mombasa. They recommended that when Miss Gem returned from her furlough, Miss Walker should be transferred to India. Later that year a letter was received from Nairobi announcing the safe arrival of Miss Walker and stating that she was settling in well. The Hostel extension was still incomplete through lack of funds.

Miss Walker wrote to the Africa Committee in London saying that she had met the Bishop of Mombasa, who recommended that YWCA work should start at the Coast as soon as possible. The Committee replied that Nairobi was the first priority.

Another letter to the Africa Committee arrived in London from a Miss Heywood commenting on "amusements allowed in the Hostel by Miss Walker" — one wonders if this lady was related to the Bishop. Maude Saunders was now apparently on the "home" staff for she was asked to reply that London did not interfere unless matters were contrary to the YWCA Constitution.

Miss Gem was expected back in Nairobi in October 1920. There is no mention as to how her furlough was arranged or financed. The Africa Committee still considered that Gertrude Walker should be posted to Madras once Miss Gem was back in the Nairobi Hostel.

In September the Africa Committee received a letter from Nairobi saying that the Committee was pleased with Miss Walker and wished her to remain. They stated that they had decided to demote Miss Gem to Bursar/Housekeeper and to reduce her salary. As Miss Gem had apparently efficiently covered all the work after the departure of Miss Saunders, this seemed very unfair. Once back in Nairobi she wrote to the Africa Committee protesting. Mrs. Ainsworth, the late President of the Nairobi Branch, was now living in England. Miss Bretherton, Secretary of World's YWCA Extension Committee, wrote to her about the matter. The Committee in London again discussed the appointment of Miss Walker to Nairobi, and it was recalled that the Candidates Committee had regarded her gifts to be in hostel work, rather than general. They considered that there was a great need for work with junior girls and Girl Guides in Nairobi, and this was not Miss Walker's forte. A letter was obviously sent to Nairobi, for in November the Nairobi President, Mrs. Gosling, wrote stating that her Committee did not see the necessity of a General Secretary in addition to a Hostel Secretary. She said that the Girl Guides were progressing independently of the YWCA. A strong letter was despatched by World's H.Q. to the Nairobi Committee condemning their treatment of Miss Gem. It would be, they said difficult to remove an impression that the Committee was inconsiderate to their staff, and that they did not want Nairobi to get a bad reputation. Maude Saunders was presumably on the Africa Committee in London for she explained that Committee members in Nairobi were constantly changing which meant that there was a danger of the principles of the YWCA being overlooked.

Presumably Miss Gem resigned, and after returning to England was employed by the YWCA in Exeter for almost two years; she was then made a very exciting offer.

1920 was the year that Kenya became a Crown colony, described in the City of Nairobi book as "...a White dominion, founded on the principles of British Traditions and Western Civilisation". The name "East African Protectorate" was discontinued and replaced by "The Colony and Protectorate of Kenya". Major General Sir Edward Northey was Governor of the Colony. Income tax was introduced. This must have affected YWCA Members but it is probable that the British system of exempting charities was adopted, which would have meant that the YWCA would not suffer.

Wives from the villages whose husbands had non-resident jobs in Nairobi were beginning to come into town, but until this year there had been no family accommodation for Africans in Nairobi. The Town Council realised that this was overdue and a very primitive housing scheme was built at Kariakor. Later this was slightly improved and a second estate was built at Shaurimoyo, the site of the demolished African village of Pangani. Some African women came to town unsupported by a family and soon the usual urbanisation problems began to materialise. As early as 1920, the Alliance of Missions started a home for the rehabilitation of prostitutes. This excellent project lasted for about ten years but had to close down through lack of funds.

War to War — 1920

1920 was also the year when cars began to replace ox-wagons, gigs and horse-drawn carriages.

The Nairobi Minutes resume in July 1921 after a break of four years.
Gertrude Walker had been Branch Secretary since April 1920.
The modified Hostel opened in l917 and extended in 1919, was fully occupied with a programme of activities functioning well. No name was given to the Hostel until l933.

It was run on the lines of a Ladies' Club with early morning tea being taken to the rooms, waiter service for lunch and dinner and a delicious afternoon tea when hot buttered scones, sandwiches and cakes were served in the lounge. It appears to have continued on much the same lines for the next 40 years, serving Europeans only.

Apparently dancing was no longer considered to be "...outside the sphere of the Association". No doubt ballroom dancing began to be accepted during the 1914-1918 war, in spite of the circular letter from World's YWCA warning Associations about "certain forms of amusement such as the dance and drama" for one of the first minutes mentions a Fancy Dress Dance held in the Hostel.

Miss Walker wrote to Miss Spencer-Smith, Correspondence Secretary of World's YWCA enclosing the Nairobi Branch subscription of Shs.20. In the letter she asked whether the Hostel belonged to the Nairobi Branch or to World's YWCA. She stressed the need for funds with which to start a hostel for girls landing in Mombasa and also a holiday and convalescent Home at the Coast.

In March the Overseas and Foreign Dept. in London received a letter from Mrs. Laws, presumably President, Nairobi Branch, saying that Miss Walker was very good but that it was too much for her to run the Hostel without a housekeeper. One wonders if this meant that the post had been vacant since the unfortunate departure of Miss Gem. London's reply was that there was a great demand for staff in Africa and that assistant staff should be recruited locally.

Mrs Gosling wrote to the London Committee in May informing them that she had resigned "...having been on the Nairobi Committee practically since its inception". Her husband had been Postmaster General and is mentioned in the early minutes on several occasions. It is not possible to determine when Mrs. Gosling first joined the Committee but from the B. O. & F. Minutes she had been President in 1920.

A Minute of the B. O. & F. Committee dated September stated that the Presidents of the YWCAs of Egypt and Palestine had recruited Miss Ethel Gem and that she would be sailing for Jerusalem in November. The Nairobi Branch did not know about this until the following January.

The first mention of a car comes in this year's Minutes. Mrs Doonholm, a Committee member, very kindly helped by transporting goods in her car. The only other way was to hire a rickshaw or station gharry which was regarded as being too expensive. The Committee therefore decided to buy a hand gharry.

A dance was held later that year at the New Stanley Hotel making a profit of Rs.1,400.

The YWCA Employment Bureau was being kept very busy so there must have been many jobs for European girls at that time in Nairobi, but "The Nairobi Jubilee History" reports that the post-war depression was beginning to take effect.

The A.G.M. was held on 31st January 1922, chaired by Lady Bowring who was now President; Mrs. Northcott was Vice-President; the Governer's wife, Lady Northey was Patron and Miss Walker was still Branch Secretary. A profit of Shs.10,000 had been made during the year. At the A.G.M. a letter was read from the Hon. Mrs Montagu Waldegrave, President World's YWCA asking for help for the Associations of Egypt and Palestine in funding a house in the Holy City, as an International Centre for women of all races and a symbol of unity in service for Christian women throughout the world. The letter states that Miss Gem, previously secretary to the YWCA in Nairobi, was in charge of this Centre. One cannot help but wonder how many of the Committee remembered Miss Gem and her untimely departure from Kenya; Miss Walker certainly did! Minutes do not say whether or not Nairobi was able to send a donation.

Apparently the E.A.W.L. was now working closely with the YWCA. Both organisations had been running Employment Bureaux in Nairobi: now the E.A.W.L. was about to close theirs, so it was very sensibly decided to run the Bureau E. A. W. L/YWCA jointly.

At the March meeting, Lady Bowring stressed the need for the E. A. W. L. and the YWCA to ensure that girls were met when they left their ships at Kilindini Harbour. Notices about the YWCA were to be posted up in all passenger liners.

Mrs. Gosling, a past President Nairobi Branch, is reported to have returned from visiting Australia where she had seen the YWCA's. work. She told the committee that the number of beds in the Australian Hostels was restricted to 40 "…to ensure a home atmosphere was retained". The Committee was interested to hear that in Australia, hostel work was usually quite separate from club activities.

Mention is now made of building a second extension to the hostel, presumably a dining room and a permanent kitchen with more bedrooms above. This would have necessitated removing the temporary structures built in 1917. Work could not be commenced until the servants' quarters had been resited and rebuilt. Further delay was caused because the Ministry of Health wrote saying that "boys" must have a room each. The committee replied asking on what authority? There appears to have been none, so work was started on the servants' quarters which again would have been a temporary structure, situated farther to the south of the Hostel. It was then possible for the extension to be built.

In April there had been what is minuted as a Native Riot Day. All the domestic staff at the Hostel had left except the "Head Boy", who must have been a brave man.

At the May meeting a letter was read from Czecho-Slovakia asking for copies of the Nairobi Annual Report and any relevant literature. The YWCA had been founded there in 1919.

A letter was read at the July meeting from London H.Q. with some criticism of the Nairobi Branch. The Secretary was asked to write for details. In October, however, Mrs. Watner, Overseas Officer, London H.Q. paid a visit to Nairobi and was apparently pleased with what she saw, for the Committee Minute states "It is a relief to know that at last a true report of Nairobi Hostel life will be taken to London H.Q.".

The Hostel was full and the Committee appeared to be opposed to any more girls coming out from England. It was felt that the YWCA should concentrate on girls already in East Africa, some with parents farming up country.

Another request for a hostel at Mombasa was received in August, but the Committee considered that Mombasa should support itself. It was decided to ask Mrs. Garland, wife of the General Manager of the African Mercantile Co., to be the YWCA Representative at the Coast, and to ask Mrs. Webb, wife of the Chief Customs Officer, to assist. In November a Mrs Jewell wrote from Mombasa saying that she did not consider that there was a pressing need for a hostel at the Coast.

A letter was read from the Salvation Army asking the YWCA to open a hostel for destitute women. The Secretary was told to reply that the Association considered that there was work for all capable women. However, by September the Committee seem to have had second thoughts and decided that a "haven" was necessary for women and girls who could not afford YWCA rates. A recommendation was sent to the Government suggesting that the present Vagrancy Regulations should be amended. Replying to the YWCA Board, Major Peel said that only as a last resort were women deported from the country.

By now repairs estimated at £2,000 were needed to the original hostel. It was decided to proceed with this work and to build a new verandah. The new extension was complete by September and reported as being habitable but not yet furnished.

A letter was received from World's YWCA in October stating that "Emissarius" was now their telegraphic address.

In November YM/YW met with representatives of local clergy to discuss whether to permit Sunday tennis. The YMCA said there was a need but hesitated to sanction it. It was therefore decided to write to London H.Q. regarding the matter.

The East African Power and Light Company was founded in 1922. Many years later this Company gave great assistance to the YWCA educational programme and opened up careers for young African Women.

The Kenya currency was now altered. Up to 1922 an East African rupee equalled Shs.1/4d. The value of the Indian rupee had increased, so, in order to relate the two currencies the East African coin was fixed at Shs.2 and became a florin. Later shillings of a size similar to the rupee, were introduced at 20 to the £.

Sir Edward and Lady Northey were about to leave the country and it was with regret that YWCA bade farewell to their Patron.

The 1923 January minutes reported that there was a typhoid epidemic in Nairobi, Miss Walker and two hostel residents were suspected of having contracted the disease. All rooms were fumigated and a dark serge curtain, which arrived from England, was hung from the east side of the verandah until sundown.

As Miss Walker was still ill in February, a cable was sent to London asking for a temporary replacement. A reply was received saying that a Mrs Morrison would be sailing for Mombasa in the "Gloucester Castle" on 22nd February. Miss Walker seems to have suddenly recovered, for a second cable was despatched which fortunately reached London in time to cancel Mrs. Morrison's passage.

The A.G.M. was held on 2nd March 1923 and Mrs Cowie was elected President. Sincere thanks were expressed to Miss Crabtree for so ably standing in as Secretary during Miss Walker's illness. The Hostel was doing well with a credit of Ksh.5,606.59. The Employment Bureau was very busy but the E.A.W.L. wished to withdraw and asked the YWCA to assume sole responsibility; this they agreed to do.

Later in March, the Governor Sir Robert Coryndon, officially opened the extension, this being the stone-built dining room and kitchens with residential accommodation above. The press reported that the opening ceremony took place in the spacious sitting room of the Hostel. This, of course, was the original building with the partition of the old dining room removed and the folding doors to the common and rest rooms thrown open, making the large lounge. Sir Robert said he hoped the YWCA would grow in usefulness with the growth of the country. Miss Walker in her address, reminded the company that it was in 1912 that the YWCA started its club work for young women, and that over the years it had grown steadily. The Hostel could now accommodate 30 with reading room, sitting room and every other attraction, all situated on the plot granted by Sir H. C. Belfield when he was Governor. It is interesting that Miss Walker gave the actual cost of the various buildings. The original Hostel had cost £1,919, the first extension which was to the north end, £548, and the present extension £3,406. Most of the latter money had been raised locally with some help from "home". Extensive renovations were still being carried out in the original part of the Hostel.

Miss Walker must have sent all this information to London for, at the April Board meeting, a letter was read from H.Q. thanking the Secretary for her interesting letter.

In May a second tennis court was planned and the existing one resurfaced. A mixed tennis tournament was organised in July. Later it was decided that gentlemen could not become members of the YWCA Tennis Club but by the end of the year it was decided that married couples could join.

Pamphlets for the new waiting room in Kilindini Harbour, Mombasa, were studied and agreed at the July meeting.

A Bridge Drive was held in the dining room with a dance in the lounge and refreshments served under the verandah. This was greatly enjoyed.

Incredible as it seems there had been a rule allowing personal servants; now this was rescinded following a letter signed by eleven residents objecting to one girl having a "personal boy"!

It was reported that rats and bats were nesting in two rooms and the architect was asked to lay traps and smoke the vermin out.

At the November meeting it was decided that there should be absolute silence in the Hostel on Sundays between 1.45 and 3.45 when the telephone was not to be answered.

This year the First Ranger Company started up in Nairobi and the YWCA offered them the use of the Hostel as their Headquarters.

Nairobi elected its first Mayor, Councillor Henderson.

During 1923 the British Colonial Office stated in effect that whilst granting self government to Southern Rhodesia, Kenya was an African territory which was not to become primarily a white colony.

By 1924 a Residents' Committee had been formed and the Minutes record a very successful Fancy Dress Ball organised by them, held in the Railway Institute. This made a profit of £30.18. Probably not for the first time and certainly not for the last, the Press reported the Ball as being organised by the YMCA!

Early in the year permission was given to Miss Lindsay, a resident, to have champagne at her wedding reception which was held in the Hostel.

At the A.G.M. held on 11th February 1924 the main business seems to have been the great need for a hostel at the Coast. Mombasa YWCA Members must have formed a committee for in May Mrs Jewell, the Chairman, asked the Nairobi Secretary to apply to the Colonial Secretary for a grant of land and to advise London about this, asking for a YWCA Secretary to be sent to Mombasa. The March minutes of Nairobi Board stated that a plot of land had been allocated to the YWCA in Mombasa and later in the year the Board received plans for a proposed hostel.

Rickshaws to Jets

Kirk Road was reported as being in very bad condition and the shamba boy was asked to fill the holes with murram. Obviously if you wanted your road repaired in those days, you had to organise it yourself.

At the July meeting it was decided to allow residents over 21 to apply for late keys; residents under 21 had to obtain permission to be out after 10.30 p.m.

In August, the Association was asked for funds towards the building of All Saints' Cathedral, to be known as the Cathedral of the Highlands. YWCA funds were scarce, so it is unlikely that the Association was able to contribute very much. Let us hope that some donation was made, for the Kenya YWCA owed a great deal to the Anglican Church and was to owe a great deal more in years to come.

The President, together with the Secretary, visited the Manager of the Standard Bank regarding the terms of the loan required to complete the payment for the 1923 extension.

At the September meeting it was agreed that the residents who did not return to the Hostel for lunch, would have their monthly account reduced by Sh. 55.

The Employment Bureau was still very busy and a Minute reads that the demand for nurses exceeded the supply.

In October a telephone was installed in the Reception Office at an annual rent of Shs.64; presumably, hitherto the only 'phone had been in the entrance hall for everyone's use. There were now two weekly newspapers in Nairobi, The Standard and The Observer.

At the November meeting, permission was given for Sunday tennis.

It will be remembered that the London H.Q. of the YMCA and the YWCA had been consulted about this in 1922.

The Secretary was asked to write to London suggesting that a Travelling Secretary be sent to Nairobi in the interest of World's YWCA, to investigate conditions in the Colony. Nairobi would offer free board and lodging.

In 1924, the Alliance of Missions co-operating with all the Protestant missions in Kenya, founded the Kenya Missionary Council which was to be the forerunner of the C.C.K.

In January 1925 the minutes reported that the YMCA had run out of sheets; a new supply was on the way from London. The YWCA came to the rescue and lent them 10 pairs! It is minuted that the YWCA rickshaw was still in use. Other sources report that there were no fewer than 200 of these conveyances in Nairobi at that time.

The A.G.M. was held on the 13th February 1925 when Mrs. Denham was elected President.

At the March meeting it was recommended that, in order to have good communication between the Hostel residents and the Hostel Committee, either a resident should attend the Hostel Committee or a member of the Hostel

War to War — 1925

Committee should go to the Residents' Meetings. In any case Minutes should be exchanged.

After the extensive repairs carried out in 1922 and 1923, it is disappointing to read that the verandah roof was leaking again.

A leader in the Mombasa Times in January had stressed that both the YMCA and the YWCA should have Hostels at the Coast.

In consequence, on the 17th March, a meeting was held at Government House, Mombasa, with the Resident Commissioner in the chair. It was decided that there were insufficient funds with which to build a hostel. A report of the meeting was sent to Nairobi and no doubt forwarded to World's YWCA.

By April the Branch Secretary, Gertrude Walker, had returned to England because of ill health and London was cabled for a replacement.

At the September meeting a letter was sent to London asking what steps other British colonies were taking regarding girls arriving from England. The E.A.W.L. and YWCA Committees decided that the Employment Bureau was so busy, it would in future, deal with YWCA members only.

Until 1921 fire prevention measures were in the hands of the Nairobi Police. In 1925 a Fire Brigade was established.

The Rev. S. E. Swann chaired the A.G.M. which was held on the 14th January 1926. Lady Grigg was elected President. The Constitution was amended to include the following: "All property, furnishings and investments to be vested in the Kenya YWCA", this being a recommendation from World's YWCA.

The March Minutes stated that the Hostel was so full that residents of more than one year were asked to find alternative accommodation, to make room for girls newly arriving in East Africa. It was decided to promote membership and the E.A.W.L. was asked for their assistance.

At the April meeting, a letter was read from World's YWCA asking Nairobi to refund the passage money of the newly arrived Secretary. It does not give her name but it must have been Miss Esse; unfortunately there is nothing in the Minutes about her arrival. As Miss Walker had left in April 1925 it would appear that Nairobi Branch was without a Secretary for almost a year. The Committee did not realise that they had accepted any responsibility towards Miss Esse's passage and Mrs Orr, who had been Chairman at the time the request for staff had been made, offered to send World's YWCA copies of all the relevant correspondence. Later in the year, it was agreed that the Nairobi Branch would endeavour to meet part of the cost of the outward voyage; money for the passage had been advanced by World's YWCA.

The June Minutes refer at length to fire precautions, and it was reported that three fluff ropes were installed at strategic points along the verandah so that residents could slide down to safety if necessary. Two Snowfire extinguishers were on order.

Rickshaws to Jets

It was now agreed that non-resident YWCA members could make use of the Library.

The November minutes state that the shamba should be re-fenced with boiler tubes from the railway and cedar posts. The cost was estimated at Shs.400. The refencing of the tennis courts had been completed.

In December it was decided to send "home" for two carpets for the big room.

The Advisory Council of the Alliance of Missions which had been established in 1918, had for eight years been endeavouring to improve and increase educational and medical facilities for Africans. 1926 was an important year, for they ratified the Constitution of the newly formed Kenya Missionary Council and opened the Alliance High School for boys at Kikuyu. It was also the year that All Saints Church became the Cathedral of the Highlands, equal in status to Mombasa Cathedral.

In February 1927, a letter was read from Eldoret asking that a YWCA Hostel should be opened there. The Secretary was instructed to reply that Nairobi would give every possible assistance but that there were no spare funds.

At the A.G.M. on the 15th February 1927 it was suggested that a hall should be built for club activities at an estimated cost of £1,800 but at the April Board meeting it was decided to borrow the Peel Memorial Hall. In May, however, it was reported that although the Peel Hall would be available, no dancing would be permitted. This Hall was, no doubt, in memory of Bishop Peel and it seems that the Church was still not in favour of dancing.

From the July Minutes we read that the Thursday Club was going well, and that a consignment of books had arrived for the library, a gift from the Victoria League. Six months later it was discovered that these were meant for the E.A.W.L. so they were faithfully delivered.

The September meeting dealt with the setting up of a Rest Room in the Hostel on the same floor as the bedrooms. This was probably for the use of non-resident members.

In November the Nairobi Corporation wrote informing the YWCA that all closets must be converted into water closets connected to the Corporation sewer. Fortunately for the Association (who were still short of funds) in December, the Corporation said there was no need to change the sewerage system at present.

The Hostel was obviously very full, for a letter to the Ministry of Education was sent advising them that the YWCA would no longer be able to continue housing their staff, but hoped to do so when the new extension was built.

November Minutes reported that the YWCA Country Dancing Team, which was part of the Thursday Club, had won a diploma at the Kenya Musical Festival.

War to War — 1928

James Smart's Jubilee History of Nairobi records that in 1927 Lady McMillan asked for a plot of land at the end of Eliot Street on which to build a Library as a memorial to her late husband, and offered to have trees planted along the street. The splendid McMillan Library was opened in 1931. For many years, Africans were not permitted to use the library.

There is a sad Minute in October saying that a Russian refugee living in the Hostel had asked if she could remain in her room. Presumably this meant that she wished to retain her room but had no money with which to pay her Hostel fees. Unfortunately there is no further mention of her; one can only hope that the YWCA was able to be of help.

Lady Denham was elected President at the A.G.M. held in the Hostel on 8th February 1928. It was resolved that a fund raising appeal should be launched to raise £4,000 with which to build an extension, presumably what came to be known as the Annex.

In February, a letter was read to the Board from Miss Evelyn Moore, Secretary to World's YWCA Training Committee regarding the 6th World's Conference which was to be held in Budapest in June. The Nairobi Branch was invited to send representatives. Regretfully no member was able to attend; probably the travel cost was too great.

At the March meeting a letter was read from the C.M.S. suggesting that an African woman be employed for upstairs work in the Hostel. The Committee, however, considered that it was "...an inopportune moment to change domestic staff". Nevertheless, they proposed that an ayah be employed to do the early morning teas and to look after sick residents. There is no way of finding out if this proposal was ever implemented. The minute, however, is of interest, because it establishes the fact that the C.M.S. was endeavouring to find employment for African women in an urban setting.

A Mrs Clarke was appointed to be the E.A.W.L. liaison member on the Committee and a YWCA member was invited to serve on the League's Committee. On June 11th an E.A.W.L./YWCA Restaurant and Restroom was opened in Nairobi; the Minutes do not state where this was situated, possibly in the Memorial Hall.

A letter was read from London H.Q. stating that £114 had been received towards the Mombasa Hostel Building Fund. The Committee decided to ask if the money in Nairobi on deposit for Mombasa could be used to rent a building as a temporary measure. In October, a letter arrived from London sanctioning this. The Committee then decided to write to the Society for Overseas Settlement for British women asking their financial assistance for the Mombasa building. They replied offering £50 once the hostel was opened! Towards the end of the year however, Mrs Usher and Mrs Gamble of Mombasa wrote to the Board saying that they considered a Mombasa hostel unnecessary.

On 14th December, a successful fund raising event took place in the form of a garden fete at Government House, Nairobi, with a cabaret in the new ballroom. The minutes do not say how much money was raised but an anonymous donation of Shs.2,589 was received.

This is the year that the Municipalities Ordinance was passed. The new Nairobi Municipal Council consisted of nine elected Europeans, seven elected Indians, two Officials nominated by Government and one Administrative Officer from Nairobi District "…to safeguard African interests".

The A.G.M. was held on 17th February 1929 when it was reported that, during 1928, there had been over 90 applications for accommodation, many of which had to be turned down. The average number of residents over the year was 25, and 5 residents had been married from the Hostel. The building fund now stood at £600.

By May the architects, Bath, Cobb & Archer, had been appointed. The new wing, which was to become known as the Annex, was to include five rooms and a bathroom. The improved sanitation in Nairobi was not yet working. The main sewer had been laid to the European School but owing to the drought there was no water pressure. Nevertheless, the new lavatory would have a water-borne system and an electric geyser for the basin; an outside water boiler would provide hot water for the new bathroom. The cost of the proposed extensions would be £1,125 excluding architects' fees of £65 which by the end of the year had risen to £88. It was estimated that the proposed electric geyser would cost Shs.60 to install and that the heating and current would cost Shs.18 per month.

The Committee decided that the new building should be insured for £1500. October minutes state that Messrs Gailey & Roberts had been asked to insure the original hostel for £10,000, thus making the total value of the building insured £11,500.

At the April Meeting, fire precautions were again discussed and it was recalled that three fluff ropes had been installed on the verandah in 1926. The Fire Service was asked to inspect again and advise. By August this had obviously been carried out because it is minuted that their recommendation was for one rope ladder, for the use of residents in rooms 7, 12 & 17. Presumably the three fluff ropes were retained.

The Hostel's leaking roof was being repaired and fund raising functions were still being organised to boost the Building Fund.

In July, a letter was received from the Acting Commissioner of Local Lands and Settlement asking whether the YWCA required any more land and in August a letter arrived from the Commissioner asking for plans of the YWCA site and buildings. In October the Association wrote saying that more land was indeed required.

In this year Mombasa became a Municipality.

War to War — 1930

1930 was an important year for World's YWCA, for they moved from 13 Grosvenor Crescent, London SW1, to Geneva.

The Nairobi Branch A.G.M. was held on 25th January 1930 and although Lady Grigg was present a Mrs Stratton was in the chair. It was reported that the overdraft of the Building Fund was Shs.9,428.99.

In May, a letter to the committee from World's H.Q. was read. It suggested that the YWCA should take up the matter of mutilation of women in Kenya. The Secretary was instructed to reply that this was outside the work of the Association and that steps were being taken by the proper authorities. This, of course, was referring to female circumcision. It seems extraordinary that World's YWCA should think that the Nairobi Branch, which had no contact at all with Africans, could have any influence on this. The Bishop of Mombasa in his March letter to the Kenya Churches Review, wrote "…female circumcision is an ancient custom and one that is very hard, even for Christian Africans, to stand against when so much social pressure is brought to bear".

Although there is nothing in the Minutes regarding the opening of the Annex, it would appear that it was occupied by August or September.

The economic depression of the 1930s was obviously beginning to hit Nairobi and the Secretary reported that many girls could not afford single rooms. By October it was decided to reduce the accommodation rates. The new single rooms in the Annex were to remain at Shs.200 per month but the single rooms in the old Hostel would be reduced to Shs.190 a month, doubles Shs 150. and cubicles Shs.125 a month. This included full board.

It would seem that the committee structure had changed over the years and that the Board had been meeting monthly and acting as the Hostel Committee, for in September the Board Minutes state that a Hostel Committee should be established and that the Board should meet quarterly.

Miss Esse, who had been Branch Secretary since 1926, was on furlough in New Zealand; the Board decided to renew her contract for a further three years. A bank draft for Shs.1,940 was sent to New Zealand. This sum was made up as follows;-

Three months salary	Shs.740
Passage N. Z.-Mombasa	Shs1100
Rail Mombasa-Nairobi	Shs.100

At the November Board Meeting a Health Insurance was set up for senior staff. This could only have meant the Branch Secretary and the Housekeeper.

The Hostel Committee reported that a new stove was to be installed in the kitchen by Thornton & Turpin at a rent of Shs.100 per month. The sink in the pantry had been recemented with a cold water tap.

Rickshaws to Jets

The 1931 January Minutes state that Messrs. Thornton and Turpin had been asked to estimate for the installation of an up-to date sanitary system including baths with hot and cold water laid on.

The A.G.M. was held on the 6th February 1931 chaired by the Rev. W. J. Wright, Dean of All Saints Cathedral. A Miss Collins was running the Thursday Club very successfully and overnight accommodation to Members was offered for Shs.seven, this included dinner, bed and breakfast.

At the March Board meeting, Lady Byrne, wife of the Governor, agreed to become President.

It was proving very difficult to persuade anyone to represent the Residents on the Hostel Committee. The idea was therefore dropped and instead, a Suggestion and Complaints box was placed in the Hostel.

Having been asked to work out the cost of food in the Hostel, the Housekeeper reported that food per head per day cost Shs.2.15. This apparently covered morning tea, cooked breakfast, cooked lunch, afternoon tea and dinner. As chickens cost only Shs.1 and meat could be bought for as little as 75 cents a pound, this is not surprising. A Mr. Bumpas offered to supply the Hostel with butter all through the year at Shs.1.50 per pound. No doubt this was accepted.

A minute reads "It was decided that one rickshaw boy should be dispensed with as the YWCA rickshaw was now rarely used."

The new sanitary system was now installed in the original hostel, including new lavatories, and bathrooms with hot and cold water, the cost being Shs.5,455.50. The old lavatories, with the partitions removed, were converted into an ironing room. As always in YWCA Hostels, residents were reminded to switch off the irons.

Lady Grigg, wife of a former Governor, and an ex-President of Nairobi YWCA now back in England, was consulted by the Nairobi Committee about the money accumulating for Mombasa. She advised that it must continue to be invested and the interest used for the YWCA work at the Coast or possibly for sending Members on holiday.

Two notice boards advertising the YWCA had been purchased for Shs.100. One was erected at the corner of the YWCA compound and the other, for the third time, at the Station; East African Railways were now going to charge a rent of Shs.60 per year.

By October Miss Esse was safely back from New Zealand where she had spent her leave.

On the 27th January 1932, The AGM was again chaired by Dean Wright. He said that 1931 had been a difficult year in the country; presumably he was referring to the recession which was affecting Britain and the whole Western World. The average number of Hostel residents had been 26 against 1930's figure of 29. Many

War to War — 1932

people in Nairobi had undergone salary cuts and this meant that some girls could not afford YWCA rates. Vacancies in the Hostel were to be advertised in the East African Standard. He said how pleased everyone was to have Miss Esse back from New Zealand.

A decision was made by the Hostel Committee that residents must not fall behind with their fees longer than two months; cases of real hardship would be considered. It was agreed that residents should be asked to leave if they were a disturbing influence in the Hostel. Rents for the Annex single rooms were reduced from Shs.200 to Shs.190 per month, single rooms in the main Hostel from Shs.125 to 120. It was reported that residents who did not return for lunch in the Hostel from Monday to Friday were receiving a rebate of Shs.20 per week. The Committee considered this was too much as it was encouraging younger residents to skip lunch. It was therefore agreed that only Shs.15 should be refunded in future.

The Minutes stated that the "Bath Boy" was to be "disposed of" now that the new bathrooms with hot and cold water were installed. Apparently the Bath Boy's duties were to carry hot water upstairs whenever a resident wanted a bath! The Minute continues "...at present there are five house boys and five bathrooms. In future each house boy will look after one bathroom". The Warden reported that residents were wasting electricity and bathing late at night. Two rules were therefore made:
1. No baths after 10 p.m.
2. Electric irons not to be used after 10 p.m.

The Committee decided that the cubicles must be reserved for girls earning £10 per month or less. The retaining fee was to be reduced from Shs.10 to Shs.5. The number of residents in the Hostel had gone down again by October but the Hostel finances were apparently still sound. The Housekeeper was asked to produce an expenditure account for food over the past six months; she was also asked to make an inventory of the linen.

A Miss Mawes, presumably a resident, had been taken ill. As there had been no room for her in the European Hospital, she had been sent to the Maia Carberry Nursing Home, the YWCA having guaranteed Dr. Burkitt that the bill would be settled. In April it is minuted that the Committee had sent a cheque for Shs.175 to cover Miss Mawes' stay in the Nursing Home.

The Hostel now had a "Wireless set" and the Committee agreed to pay half the licence fee of Shs.100 per year, the other Shs.50 to be paid by residents; a box was to be placed in the Hostel for donations.

The December meeting was an historic one for the Minutes record that the YWCA cable address was no longer necessary as Airmail was now available. Some National Associations, however, continued to retain the cable address in the World Directory.

Rickshaws to Jets

At the A.G.M. on 20th January 1933 Mrs Moore was elected President. The Hostel had been running for sixteen years, and extended on three occasions, but was still referred to as 'The Hostel'. In 1933, the name Windsor House was chosen, Windsor being the name which the British Royal Family had adopted during the 1914-18 war, in place of their Germanic name. The YWCA address was therefore in "Windsor House, Kirk Road, Nairobi".

Mrs Betty Galton-Fenzi, an Australian by birth, had been a Committee Member for some years and the March minutes record that she was welcomed back from a holiday in U.K. Her husband was a founder member of the Corydon Museum, and in 1919 he also founded the Royal East African Automobile Association, later to become the A. A. of Kenya. In 1926 he, together with Mr P. Gethin, were the first people to drive a car from Mombasa to Nairobi. The "road", in those days, went via Taveta near the Tanganyika border and the journey took them three weeks. The car was a Riley Redwing, registration number B3. During this epic run, the tyres punctured no less than 52 times!

By now, residents were beginning to own cars and a garage for five cars was built at the cost of £40. The Branch Secretary, Miss Esse, was allocated £1 a month for petrol and the running expenses of her car.

Miss Picton-Tushwell, a former World YWCA Vice-President had called at the YWCA during a visit to Kenya.

The Forestry Department was asked to cut down some of the gum trees in the garden. The next Minute states that briquettes were to be used for cooking instead of wood; perhaps the YWCA wood was too damp.

In November it was decided to send details of Windsor House to the clergy in charge of Mombasa Cathedral, to advertise in Nakuru, and to continue the weekly advertisement in the Nairobi press.

The A.G.M., held on 16th February 1934, was again chaired by Dean Wright. Mrs Moore was still President of the Nairobi Branch and she welcomed Lady Byrne, wife of the Governor. Mrs Galton-Fenzi was re-elected to the Board. Miss Esse's Report was rather dismal. The balance sheet showed a deficit of Shs.7,000. Some residents were still unable to pay full fees and were being accommodated at reduced rates; several bad debts had been written off. It was pointed out that as one of the objects of the YWCA was to relieve poverty, the Association's aim was being achieved. It was nevertheless essential that running expenses be met. She said that the Association in Kenya was entirely self supporting with no help from "home". On the brighter side, there had been many casual visitors — from China, India, Egypt, South Africa and England. A member of staff from London H.Q. had resided in the Hostel for several months. Unfortunately no name is given. The Report continues that the Nairobi Ranger Company was meeting regularly in Windsor House Lounge, some residents being Rangers. The Hostel

War to War — 1934

dropped during the year from Shs.47,049 to Shs.33,675, but expenditure had also been reduced. She said that conditions in Nairobi were rapidly changing and it was important that the YWCA kept pace with these changes. The President thanked Miss Esse for her Report and expressed appreciation to her and Mrs Crawford, the Housekeeper.

Later in February, an order from the Central Revenue Office arrived stating that Windsor House must take out a licence under the Licensing Ordinance. A letter was drafted to the Colonial Secretary giving the full aims and objects of the YWCA and asking that the matter be brought to the notice of the Governor. It was hoped that H.E. would endeavour to grant an exemption of the Licence Fee. In April, the matter of the Licensing Ordinance 1933 was again discussed. The Governor had indeed appealed on behalf of the YWCA but had not been successful; a further appeal was to be made. By July, however a letter was received from the Secretariat stating that the Licensing Commission had agreed to exempt the YWCA from the Licensing Ordinance 1933 in respect of twelve beds. The Association would be required to pay the Licence for sixteen beds only: the Hostel's full quota was 28 to 30 beds.

By the March Meeting, the Bank Balance was down to Shs.950 so it was with gratitude that a donation of Shs.100 was received from Mrs Bastard of an old established Kenya family which was still living in the country at the time this book was written.

In May, the Minutes state that rooms 15 and 16 had been made into cubicles and Hostel rates were to be reduced as follows:

Annex single rooms Shs.170. per month; single rooms in Windsor House Shs.150 per month, doubles Shs.130 and cubicles Shs.117. The rebate to residents who chose not to take lunch in the Hostel was to be discontinued.

The Committee decided that all the electric wiring should be tested. Following this, the Fire Master carried out an inspection and was satisfied that the residents were protected in every way.

It was reported that" strange natives" had been attempting to enter the building at night: the police had been called. The Committee decided that residents should be given keys and all outside doors should be locked at dinner time. Expanded metal was to be put on the Housekeeper's windows which were on the ground floor.

Thos. Cook, the Travel Agent, had agreed to include the YWCA on their list of hotels and boarding houses.

The E.A.W.L. kindly allowed YWCA members to use their Rest Room in the Memorial Hall free of charge. Does this mean that the joint Restroom/Restaurant opened in 1928 was now entirely an E.A.W.L. project?

A letter was received from Charlotte Niven, General Secretary World's YWCA asking for a statement about the £114 collected in 1928 in England in response to an appeal by Lady Grigg for the proposed Mombasa Hostel. The Secretary was asked to reply that the money was on fixed deposit with the Standard Bank of South Africa. She was told to explain that, as there was no prospect of a hostel in Mombasa at present, it was hoped that World's YWCA would allow the money to be used as an Emergency Fund by the Nairobi Branch. Some months later a reply came from Miss Niven stating that her Committee could not give permission for Nairobi to use any of the Mombasa funds. Her suggestion was that it might be made into a holiday fund for girls who could not afford to visit the Coast; this had been suggested in 1931 by Lady Grigg. The Secretary was told to reply that, as the railway fare was exorbitant and board and lodging at the Coast very "high", the Committee had decided to keep the fund on fixed deposit.

Lady Rhodes was invited to join the Board. Miss Esse asked to extend her tour for an additional year to 1935, in order to avoid the English winter. Her request was granted.

The Board met in January 1935 and Lady Rhodes agreed to become President. Mrs. Nicholson and Mrs Galton-Fenzi were asked to look into the food expenditure. It was stated that the building needed some repair, and Lady Rhodes, whose husband was in charge of the Railways, said that she would ask for a Railway employee to advise the Hostel Committee.

At the A.G.M. on 26th February 1935 Canon Wingfield-Digby was in the chair. Lady Rhodes' appointment as President was confirmed. A programme was arranged as follows: 5-6 p.m. Tea in the lounge followed by songs by Miss Bullock; piano solo by Mrs. Gledhill; five minutes sketch called 'Lucky Jim' by Miss Barber, Miss Harrison and Mr. Luckham.

We must hope that this concert cheered people up for Lady Rhodes, in her Presidential address, said that the Hostel Report was not good. The average number of residents over the year had been eighteen, about twelve of whom were young girls taking various training courses in Nairobi. Consequently, the less expensive cubicles had been in great demand. The residents were enjoying their wireless set, and a gift of 54 gramophone records had been gratefully received. Thanks were expressed to the East African Standard for their assistance with publicity, and to the Auditors, Messrs Dunn & Thornby. Special thanks were expressed to Miss Esse for her unfailing devotion.

The Secretary was asked to write to the "The Kenya Weekly News", the weekly edition of "The East African Standard" and the "Uganda Herald", giving information to up-country people, about YWCA accommodation, and activities in Nairobi. It is interesting to note that the Association was again endeavouring to involve the daughters of European settlers in YWCA activities, with less emphasis on the needs of girls arriving from U.K.

War to War — 1935

At their March Meeting, the Board agreed to pay for a 3rd class passage to England for the Housekeeper on condition that she would return after six months if required, but by October a Mrs. Marshall had been appointed as Housekeeper.

In April, in spite of the acute shortage of money, mosquito nets for every bedroom were purchased and a new tennis court net was bought. It was now realised that bed linen was as cheap in Nairobi as it was in England, so in future, purchases would be made locally.

The July Minutes state that a resident had contracted typhoid. All residents were inoculated; the Government Laboratory was asked to do this free of charge. It was noted that the waste land near the Hostel had not been cleared and a letter was therefore to be sent to the Municipal Health Dept.

In September the Hostel Current Account was down to Shs.1,089 and it was therefore necessary to transfer funds from the Fixed Deposit Account. There were only nine residents so it was decided to advertise the Hostel on Nairobi cinema screens.

A letter was received from the Revenue Officer reminding the Association that exemption granted by the Licensing Ordinance had been for 1934 only and did not apply to 1935. Lady Rhodes agreed to write to the Deputy Governor giving the Association's Profit and Loss Account for the last 18 months. There must have been great relief at the November meeting, for Mr. Walsh, Tax Revenue Officer, had agreed to exempt the YWCA for 1935. Shortly afterwards, a letter was received from the Chairman of the Licensing Commission stating that the YWCA was "…outside the scope of the Licensing Ordinance 1933 and therefore not subject to duty". What a waste of time and paper this bureaucratic muddle had entailed and what unnecessary worry it had caused.

By now, an Indian Maternity Hospital was in operation and, in 1935, an antenatal and children's clinic was built in the grounds.

This was the year of King George V and Queen Mary's Silver Jubilee, and six days of festivities were organised which included processions of decorated cars and lorries, tree planting and fireworks. On Wednesday of that week, the new Law Courts and Town Hall were officially opened, replacing the former buildings which had been constructed of wood and iron.

The A.G.M. held on 24th January 1936 was organised as in 1935, tea being served to guests on arrival, followed by a concert which preceded the meeting. Dean Wright was in the chair. Lady Rhodes in her Presidential Report explained that since the YWCA opened its first Hostel in Kenya at Bishopsbourne in 1913, many boarding houses and hotels had opened making accommodation in Nairobi more available, but there was still a need for hostel accommodation for girls starting life in Nairobi, some working, others in training. She stressed that up-country people could not afford high prices. "The town could be a very lonely

Rickshaws to Jets

place" she said, "and it made a great difference to a girl, newly arrived in Nairobi, to be met with a spirit of comradeship. The essential function of the YWCA hostel was to be a real home for girls."

Apparently people were so short of money at this time, that many in and around Nairobi were taking paying guests, which of course took income from the YWCA.

It is interesting to note the prices of the time: the United Dairies were supplying the Hostel with butter at Shs.1.10 per lb. and milk at Shs.1.10 per gallon.

At the March meeting, it was reported that Windsor House roof was leaking again; this was a repair which the Hostel could ill afford at that time. Appealing for money was still a major activity and a letter was sent to Lady Byrne asking if she and H.E. would lend Government House for a fund raising function. Miss Kirby, Head Mistress of the Girls Secondary School, kindly gave permission for the school premises to be used during the holidays, and dances and whist drives were held there. Cable & Wireless installed a "wireless plant" and Lady Rhodes arranged for the Railways to supply an amplifier.

The buildings and contents were revalued for insurance as follows:

Buildings £6,000
Furniture and fittings £1,000

This reduction of £4,500 since 1929 seems excessive but was, no doubt, due to the World recession and depreciation of buildings and furnishings.

Dr. McCaldine accepted the position of Medical Adviser to the YWCA. The Secretary was requested to write and ask if he would treat hostel residents and staff at a reduced rate; he kindly agreed to reduce his fees by 25 per cent.

The British Council was not established in Nairobi until 1947 but in 1936 they offered to supply the YWCA with magazines from Britain.

When a letter was received from World's YWCA asking for funds, the reply was that the Branch regretted that they had no money. Lady Rhodes suggested that everyone on the Board should endeavour to bring in five new members.

A strange minute reads "The Minute Book must be brought to every meeting".

The AGM was held on 25th January 1937 and chaired by Dean Wright; the meeting was again preceded by tea and a concert. He spoke very appreciatively of the YWCA in Kenya "...at a time when it was armed with revolvers". Extensive research has taken place in an attempt to ascertain what this extraordinary minute could have meant. But even people living in Nairobi at that time were unable to give any explanation except to say that there was the beginning of some political unrest which was put on hold during the war. Miss Heron, a visitor to Nairobi, said that she had stayed in YWCA hostels in many parts of the world and that the one in Nairobi was as good as any she had come across.

Mr. Cleland of Queens Hotel offered the YWCA the use of his hotel for a fund raising event, suggesting either a sundowner dance or an evening dance. He

War to War — 1937

kindly agreed to supply ices and coffee free of charge. The Committee gratefully accepted and decided to hold a dance which should start from 9 to 10 pm. The dance was a success making a profit of just over Shs.380.

An added expense which the Association could ill afford at this time was caused by the Hostel being struck by lightning. The damage was repaired by the E.A.P.&L., the work costing just over Shs.840. Fortunately the Y.WC.A. Insurance Policies covered this and Shs.840 was reimbursed by the agent of Messrs. Gailey & Roberts. As a precaution, however, a lightning conductor was installed costing approximately Shs.380, exactly the profit of the dance!

The YMCA in Nairobi had closed down in 1936 and their building taken over by TOC H. Apart from work with the Armed Forces during the second World War, they did not operate in Nairobi again until 1952 when their present centres were opened. Lady Brook-Popham, the Governor's wife, said that there were still books in the YMCA Library which she could procure for the YWCA.

The November Minutes state that a Housekeeper was suddenly needed; it doesn't say why. Mrs F. Thomson, who had been at Limuru Girls' School for two and a half years, was taken on temporarily.

Sympathy was expressed to Mrs Galton-Fenzi on the death of her husband. This is recorded, as Mrs Galton-Fenzi had been serving on the Committee since 1929 and continued to serve for many years. She figures again as Patron at the end of this story.

A fund raising organ recital was given at All Saints Cathedral resulting in a £10 donation to the Association.

On 17th February 1938, the Rev. J. H. Ogilvie chaired the A.G.M. The Rt. Rev. R. T. Crabbe, who had become Bishop of Mombasa in 1936, was also present. 1937 had been a good year for the Hostel which was then full, preference being given to girls newly arrived in East Africa and to young daughters of up-country parents.

It seems that Lady Brooke-Popham, wife of the Governor, was now President, for the Board met at Government House in May.

A large Blue Triangle was erected on the corner by the tennis courts, at the junction of Kirk and Protectorate Roads, and it was decided that the notice at the railway station should be put in a more prominent position.

A letter was read to the Hostel Committee from Mr. Meredith Powell saying that he objected to his daughter being told that she must be in by 10. 30 p.m., stating that she was a very responsible and trustworthy girl. The Secretary was told to reply that Hostel Rules could not be broken, explaining that many residents were young girls away from home for the first time, whose parents relied on the YWCA to take good care of them.

Two residents were on very low salaries, earning Shs.100 and Shs.160 per month respectively. As their Hostel bills were Shs.100 and Shs.115, they had asked for a reduction. It was decided to write to their parents who apparently lived up-country and if it were a matter of genuine poverty, their Hostel rates would be reduced to Shs.90 and Shs.100.

It was decided that the linen room should be converted into a drying room and room 26, which led out of the lounge, should become a linen room. A handsome clock had been presented to the Hostel. The Bank Balance now being Shs.9,802, it was decided to transfer Shs.5,000 back to the fixed deposit.

The Secretary was asked to write to the S.O.S.B.W. and enquire if they would be prepared to contribute towards the building of extra rooms to be reserved for girls arriving in Kenya.

Mrs Galton-Fenzi was in the chair at the November meeting and she was thanked for bringing beautiful flowers for the Hostel. A hot water boiler had been installed in the staff bathroom, and a lavatory in the upstairs bathroom. It was decided that girls under 16 should not be encouraged to become residents. Miss Esse was due for six months leave after a term of four years. The Committee invited her to return for another three years. This she agreed to accept. Mrs. Thomson, the temporary Housekeeper was reported as being very satisfactory.

The December Minutes report that a German resident, aged 17, had been asked to leave as she could not pay her rent. She would be returning to her parents in Tanganyika which, until 1917 had been German East Africa. At the end of the First World War it became a protectorate under the League of Nations to be administered by the British Government.

Plans for Christmas were discussed and every resident was allowed to bring one friend, free, on Christmas Day.

It appears that the Referee System, set up in 1914, had been abandoned for it was now decided to invite up-country women from Rongai, Njoro, Kitale and Subukia to be ex-officio members of the Board, and the Principal of the Kenya Girls' High School was also invited to serve. Mombasa was of course already represented. A letter had been received from the Commissioner of Lands asking why the YWCA required more land and when building was likely to commence. The Secretary was asked to reply that an extension was very necessary but that the Association had only £1,000 in the building fund.

When in 1935 Charlotte Niven retired as World's General Secretary she had been succeeded by Ruth Woodsmall who now wrote to Nairobi asking for an update report of YWCA activities. After discussion, the Board decided to confine the report to Windsor House residents and visitors and "…not to mention Mombasa at this stage".

Lady Delamere was elected Mayor of Nairobi, the first woman to hold this office.

The Colonial Government Health Department was way ahead of the local YWCA for it decided to build a group hospital to serve all races. Unfortunately the outbreak of war the following year delayed this splendid plan.

War to War — 1939

Education for Africans was still very inadequate. The S.P.K. book "Rabai to Mumias" states that in 1938 only 12 per cent of African children attended school.

Apparently Mrs. Galton-Fenzi was now President. At the January 1939 meeting a Christmas greeting was read from the H.Q. of the YWCA in New Zealand, no doubt because of Miss Esse's recent visit.

The A.G.M. was held on the 18th April 1939 with Canon Wingfield-Digby in the chair. The meeting was again preceded by tea and a musical programme. It was reported that The Kenya War Emergency Organisation had been set up; this seems rather premature.

The Hostel Committee decided that, as the Bank Balance was now Shs.8,408.30, another Shs.5,000 should be put on fixed deposit. The residents had produced two short plays at a farewell party given for the Housekeeper, Mrs Barclay, and a welcome back to Miss Esse. Tennis was very popular and the two courts in great demand. Several tennis matches had been played between the YWCA and local schools and a mixed tennis tournament had been held lasting four days. Mrs Galton-Fenzi presented the prizes.

The April minutes state that the S.O.S.B.W. were not always taking up the rooms reserved for them. It was therefore decided that in future a booking fee should be charged. The Hostel was full to overflowing and girls were being turned away. It was urgent that a new wing be built.

In June food poisoning was a scare in Nairobi but there is no mention of cases in the Hostel. A new typewriter was purchased; unfortunately no price was mentioned.

At the July meeting a new rule was made that girls under 18 years of age must ask permission if they wished to go out at night.

By September, the Second World War had begun. Five residents had already been called up. The Committee discussed Air Raid Precautions and it was decided that the dining room was the best place for an Air Raid Shelter. However, by October it was decided that two trenches should be dug in the garden, one for the Hostel staff and residents and the other for "native" staff.

A letter was received from the Government Land Department confirming that an adjacent plot had been granted to the Association.

Mrs. Galton-Fenzi was in the chair at the November meeting when it was decided to put a further Shs.2,000 on fixed deposit. The Minutes state that there were Americans and Czecho-Slovakians staying in the Hostel which was still full. The S.O.S.B.W. wrote offering financial help for the building of new rooms to be reserved for their members. It was however decided to delay further building until after the war.

Towards Integration
1940 — 1954

The war in Europe necessitated World's YWCA opening a temporary office in Washington. To the Geneva H.Q. were assigned the special functions of maintaining contact with Associations in Continental Europe and of organising aid to the fast mounting number of refugees. To the Washington Office was transferred responsibility for the work of the Executive Committee. Miss Marianne Mills was placed in charge of this office and, in Ruth Woodsmall's absence, acted in her stead.

Miss Esse reminded the Committee that she was sent out by London to be General Secretary, Nairobi Branch, but seeing the growing importance of the Hostel, she was willing to be Honorary Secretary to the Hostel as well. A request was made for a telephone extension. This was refused as there was no equipment in the country. However the secondhand electric refrigerator was replaced by a new one.

The Italians were now in the war, having joined Germany against Britain and her Allies. A total blackout was enforced in Kenya and Nairobi expected air raids by the Italian Air Force based in Somalia. One of their planes did fly over the town but dropped no bombs. Far more danger came from the lions who, appreciating the lack of street lighting, and being able to see in the dark, made nightly raids on Nairobi dustbins.

Although in October 1939 it was decided that no further building should take place during the war, Minutes of March 1941 state that the new stone built Boys' quarters had been completed. These were probably located near the existing temporary quarters which were on the site where the lower income hostel was later to be built. As in 1938 the Commissioner of Lands had asked when building was likely to commence; the Board, very probably thought it diplomatic to put up some permanent construction on the newly acquired plot. They had a limited sum in the building fund so it must be assumed that stone built servants' quarters was the scheme on which they decided.

In June a second hand typewriter was purchased for Shs.400. 00.

The Minutes now record that Miss Esse stated that she wished to resign in September; no reason was given. She had been back from long leave for only two years. Her departure must have created a great gap in the life of the Nairobi Association for she had been Branch Secretary for over fifteen years and from the little that can be gleaned from the Minutes, she was extremely capable, hard working and popular. A letter was sent to London asking for permission to recruit a Hostel Secretary locally. A Miss Shaw was appointed temporarily for three months.

Towards Integration — 1942

A cable had been received from London asking for volunteers to join the British YWCA War Services. Young women were urgently needed to run Service Clubs in the Middle East. The Headquarters of the British War Services in Cairo was headed by a remarkable New Zealand woman whose name is now famous in YWCA circles– Jean Begg, affectionately known as J. B. She had been working for the World's YWCA for many years based in India and at that time she was General Secretary of India, Burma and Ceylon. In 1939, Minutes of the British Overseas and Foreign Committee stated that she was due for 18 months leave and it was suggested that after her furlough in New Zealand she should return to India to train an Indian N.G.S., and no doubt local women for Burma and Ceylon. It was whilst she was on leave that World's YWCA recommended her to Great Britain for the important War Service Post. Three people, well known to older members in Kenya, were on her staff in Egypt -Isabel Catto, Doreen Boedeker (nee) Lance, and Vera Harley.

At the 1942 A.G.M. the Rt. Rev. H. T. Crabbe, Bishop of Mombasa, was in the chair. Miss Ripley, apparently recruited locally, had been appointed secretary for the Hostel. A letter was received from the Government reminding the YWCA that building on the newly acquired plot should be started within two years of receiving the Land Grant. Now that the country was at war, this was going to be difficult, if not impossible. There is no minute reminding the Government that already stone quarters had been built for the servants.

The 1939/45 War brought changes to the YWCA all over the world. For the first time in British history, girls were conscripted to serve in the Forces and many were posted overseas, some, of course, to Kenya. Lady Churchill, then "Mrs", was Chairman of the British YWCA War Services and in 1942 she broadcast on the B. B. C. appealing for funds, saying "Being a mother myself, I know how you mothers must be feeling when your daughters are posted overseas to serve with the Army, Navy and Air Force. But don't worry, the YWCA is there and will take care of them."

More and more service women arrived in Kenya and by 1943 the accommodation problem became acute. Windsor House and the Annex were already full so the YWCA were unable to assist except by allowing the Army to build two wooden huts in the forecourt of Windsor House. The smaller one had five bedrooms and the larger could accommodate twelve: both had adequate bathroom facilities.

Many of the service women were employed in Command establishments in the town. These women were accommodated in various camps, one near Government House, another near Kenton College and some were in Loreto Convent. The Municipal Hostel in Portal St. was taken over by the Inner Wheel as a hostel for service women.

In Mombasa the same accommodation problem existed, mainly for Wrens. The Royal Navy therefore commandeered a makuti building halfway along Cliff Avenue. This served as a small hostel and club for service women at the Coast and was run by the Women's United Service Club. There is little doubt that local YWCA members were involved in this venture, as this history will reveal.

A letter was read at the April Committee meeting in Nairobi from the Navy Office expressing gratitude to the YWCA for entertaining naval personnel on leave from the Coast. From this it would seem that the Nairobi Branch had been organising entertainment for the forces before the official YWCA War Services was set up in Kenya.

The July Minutes report that there was an improvement in the Saturday night dances which apparently took place in the Lounge, though still "...a few girls come dressed in their office cotton frocks". Obviously, Committee members would have preferred all the Residents to be smartly dressed.

The C.C.K. was founded on August 7th and they offered books on subscription to the YWCA Library. It is interesting to read from the Minutes that the Christian Science Monitor was gratefully accepted. This publication is referred to again later.

At the October meeting, Mrs Jackie Taffs of the British YWCA War Services is first mentioned. It would appear that she was either an Australian or a New Zealander for in 1939 the minutes of the British Overseas and Foreign Department record that she was due for home leave from India. They gave her instructions to travel first to London to report to the Committee and then to proceed home via America. She had been on the YWCA staff in Madras as far back as the 1920s, where she would have been working with Jean Begg, who no doubt, persuaded her to join the British War Service Staff and had subsequently seconded her from Cairo to set up the Service work in Nairobi. She told the Committee about the welfare being organised by Jean Begg's staff for Service personnel in Asmara, Egypt, North Africa, Iraq, Iran and Palestine. She pointed out that any wartime measure of the YWCA would lay the foundation for expansion after the war.

Early in 1944, a letter was received from Mrs. Norman in Mombasa saying that there was no need for a hostel at the Coast but that a club room was very necessary and this should be followed by a hostel after the War. The makuti building was obviously meeting the accommodation needs.

There had been Italian prisoners of war in Kenya since 1941, probably from the War zone in Abyssinia. By 1944, some were working for the YWCA and it was they who terraced the Hostel garden and planted a productive vegetable shamba. Petrol was now very short, for the residents' garage was converted into a cycle shed.

At the meeting of the Board of Management on the 7th March, there was some confusion between the local YWCA and the YWCA War Services. Jackie Taffs

Towards Integration — 1945

explained that the War Services was entirely a war-time operation, quite separate from the civilian YWCA. It had been set up to serve women in the Forces only. She assured the Committee, however, that properties belonging to the War Services would eventually be handed over to the local Association; this probably referred to the two wooden buildings mentioned previously and later to be known as the "pre fabs". The Committee seem to have been reassured for they offered to give every assistance to Mrs Taffs and Miss Violet MacDonnell. Violet, known as Judy, who had been locally recruited from Limuru, was the youngest of Mr and Mrs A. B. MacDonnell's four daughters. He had arrived in Limuru in 1907 and was the first person in East Africa to grow tea. This was not his only claim to fame: he designed and helped to build Limuru Church and in 1922 founded Limuru Girls' School. Limuru is agriculturally interesting for it is situated at the altitude where coffee no longer grows and where tea begins.

During this year, Doreen Lance was transferred by Jean Begg from Eritrea to Kenya to take over from Jackie Taffs as Director of YWCA work with women of the Allied Forces. She travelled via H.Q. Cairo where incidentally she met Isabel Catto and Vera Harley. Judy MacDonnell volunteered to join Jean Begg's team in Cairo, where she worked with Isabel and Vera. Although there is no mention in the Minutes of Jean Begg having visited Kenya, she must have done so for Judy's parents remembered her going to see them in Limuru, and Sir Godfrey Rhodes, who was in charge of all transport in Kenya during the war, was still in touch with her in 1958 as this history later reveals.

It was during this year that Mr. E. W. Mathu, the first Kenya African to graduate from Oxford, was nominated as an Unofficial Member of the Legislative Council.

Unfortunately there is now a gap in the Minutes until 1952 but with the help of the Nairobi Jubilee book, and World's YWCA. archives, it has been possible to glean a little information.

In 1945 Doreen Lance married Frank Boedeker, a coffee farmer in Kabete, son of a Nairobi doctor. After the War Services closed down, Doreen resigned from the staff but always kept in touch with the YWCA.

On May 8th 1945 "V.E. Day", a flag day was held in aid of the Kenya Women's Emergency Organisation Comforts Fund and Red Cross Services. The YWCA was probably involved both in assisting and, hopefully, in receiving from this.

Many Africans had served in the British Armed Forces, and many had lost their lives. No doubt this helped to break down racial barriers for it was in 1946 that the first two Africans took their seats on the Nairobi Municipal Council. In Anna Rice's book "A History of the World YWCA" it is stated that in 1946 East Africa was considered to be one of the areas with particular opportunities for development.

The only information available in 1947 is in a letter, dated 31st August, to World's YWCA from Phyllis Doveton Sturder Macquarie, who had been Nairobi

Branch Secretary since 1st June. From this we learn that Mrs. Foster-Sutton, wife of the Acting Governor, was acting as the YWCA President. It appears that the President was Betty Galton-Fenzi, who had now remarried and was Mrs. Montgomery. She was temporarily out of the country. The Hostel was staffed by a Housekeeper, and a Night Matron and there were 49 girls in residence. It would seem that the "pre-fabs" were already in use for extra accommodation.

There is a memo in World's YWCA files setting out what was happening in Mombasa. Once all the Wrens and other Service women had left, the Royal Navy had handed over the makuti building to the local YWCA Committee. The memo continues, "...Money is urgently required for the hostel building fund and later a General Secretary will be needed".

The Jubilee History of Nairobi states that every ship from South Africa and the U.K. brought would-be settlers.

In August, the first Industries Show was organised by the Town Council; this stimulated pride in African crafts and for the first time it was realised that the skill of the Kikuyu and the Wakamba was not limited to domestic work and driving.

Towards the end of the year the E.A.W.L. was having a European Child Welfare Clinic built at Parklands, and, at Muthaiga, a children's Hospital. This hospital was financed by Colonel Grogan in memory of his late wife, and called after her — Gertrude's Garden.

Until this year, only a very limited number of African girls had been given the opportunity of education up to School Certificate standard; a few places were allocated to girls in the Alliance Boys' High School. In 1947 the first secondary school for girls was founded at Kikuyu — The African Girls' High School, later to become the Alliance Girls' School.

In 1948 discussions were taking place by the Kenya War Memorial Management Committee as to the form Nairobi's Memorial should take. It was eventually decided that it should be incorporated in the all-races Cultural Centre, having in the foyer a special feature bearing the names and regiments of those who had fallen. The site of the Cultural Centre, renamed The Kenya Institute, was in the fork of Sadler Street and Government Road; this necessitated constructing pavements in Sadler Street. Roads in Nairobi were being generally improved and traffic islands built. An important development was the founding of the East African Literature Bureau, part of its work being a library service for Africans and the training of Africans as professional librarians.

Plans were afoot to increase Nairobi's water supply. A dam was to be constructed to hold 1,000,000,000 gallons of the storm flow of the Chania and the Sasumua Rivers. This would cost £750,000 and would augment the town's daily water supply by 4,000,000. gallons. This was expected to be completed by 1952.

Towards Integration — 1948

Nothing can be found about the YWCA in Kenya with the exception of a letter to the World's YWCA from Mrs L. Challoner-Davies, Chairman YWCA Mombasa, written from Cliff Avenue. She was, of course, writing from the newly acquired makuti building now belonging to the YWCA. She stated that the Hostel had been running at a loss for some time but was now paying its way. The land on which the makuti Hostel stood belonged to the Education Department and the Government offered to buy the building from the YWCA for £3,000. Mrs Challoner-Davies explained that the plans which had been produced for the new Hostel had been too ambitious, costing twice the amount the Committee felt they could afford. The Architect had therefore modified the drawings, and plans were going ahead to build accommodation for thirty residents and two staff, thus reducing the cost by half to £8,000. That meant that the Association had to find £5,000.

Fund raising was in progress and Mrs Challoner-Davies said that a Hostel Secretary would be required in 1949. If she was hoping to receive financial help she certainly went about it in the wrong way, for the letter continues "A YWCA is not what is wanted here; what is required is a Women's Hostel, Club Type". In October a reply was dispatched from the International Secretary, Geneva, stating that her Committee would more favourably consider helping a centre which would be serving girls of all sections of the community; they had, she said "...very definite views about YWCAs which were serving Europeans only". The letter concluded by saying that Miss Marianne Mills of World's YWCA staff would be visiting Kenya the following January, and the Mombasa Branch should make a point of discussing their problems with her.

Early in 1949 the E.A.W.L. sponsored a conference at the Town Hall in Nairobi, of women's organisations in Africa. There can be little doubt that the YWCA were involved.

Marianne Mill was a senior member of World's YWCA having joined the staff in 1926. During the war, when the World's Office had been divided between Geneva and Washington, she had frequently stood in for the World's General Secretary. No account of her visit to Kenya can be found, but it is certain that she was in the country in January 1949, for in subsequent letters, she is mentioned with appreciation and affection.

Although Doreen Boedker was no longer connected with the Branch in Nairobi, it seems that, during her visit, Miss Mills made a point of seeing her. They had known each other during the 1930s when Doreen was working for the YWCA in England before joining Jean Begg's War Service team in l941. Soon after Miss Mills returned to Geneva she received a letter from Doreen saying how much she would like to work for the YWCA again. Marianne replied "My dear Doreen, Nairobi has been asking for an experienced worker for two years and no one suitable has been found. It seems a pity when you are there and available."

Doreen was hardly "available" as she and her husband were running a coffee farm at Kabete.

It is obvious that Miss Mills' visit was a great success and that she formed a good relationship with Nairobi Branch President, Mrs Betty Montgomery. Soon after she returned to Geneva, Miss Helen Roberts, who was now World's General Secretary, wrote in some distress to the Nairobi President saying that she had been sent a press cutting from the "Mombasa Times" which stated that in December a tombola had been held to raise funds for the new hostel; she says she is "very troubled". She had been given to understand that the C.C.K. were against such things. Fortunately, Miss Mills had assured her that the YWCA group in Mombasa were fine, public spirited people and "…she feels sure that with your help they would want to bring their work in line with the YWCA aim and purpose." It would be interesting to know how Betty Montgomery handled this!

Soon afterwards, a letter arrived for Mrs Montgomery from Miss Mills in which she says "It is essential that Mombasa know the kind of Movement into which they are coming and the principles which must be given to the work if it is to be a YWCA." It appears that Marianne also mentioned having heard from Doreen, because a subsequent minute states that Mrs Boedeker had been invited to join the Nairobi Committee.

Mrs. Montgomery was certainly an active and hard-working President, frequently sending long hand written letters to Geneva and London. On August 18th, she wrote to Mrs. French in Geneva saying that she felt sure that Miss Mills would have told her that the Nairobi Hostel was going well with a good Committee and that the Bishop of Mombasa was very enthusiastic. The Branch had been fund raising and £50 had been sent to the Mombasa Building Fund.

Probably referring to her recent discussions with Miss Mills regarding the possibility of expanding the work to include Africans she said "Big changes must come slowly — the right moment suddenly appears, especially when one has given a subject particular thought." She concluded by stressing the need for a trained worker who would be capable of carrying out new programmes.

The Anglican Church was determined to find the money with which to complete the Cathedral and a fund raising appeal was launched.

1950 was a year of great importance to Nairobi for, on 30th March, the town was granted City Status. Nairobi was by then the largest town in East Africa, an international communications centre for trade and diplomatic missions and a powerful financial base. A beautiful Coat of Arms was designed for the new City at the foot of which is the motto in Swahili "Shauri kwa Uaminifu" which translated means "Let us conduct our deliberations faithfully with diligence."

On July 10th Mrs Boedeker wrote to Miss Roberts saying how glad she was to be on the Committee after a lapse of four years. From this letter it would appear that Doreen had never met Helen Roberts for she tells her that during her training

Towards Integration — 1951

in the 1930s, she had spent a year at the YWCA College at Selly Oak, Birmingham. There, she had particularly enjoyed the experience of being with students of all races and since then had always been interested in the international side of the Association. She goes on to say that she hopes to be able to make a contribution to club work in Nairobi and to the development of international understanding. She concluded by telling the World's General Secretary, that a Red Cross Detachment had been formed by hostel residents. Like the YWCA, the Red Cross in Kenya was still entirely European.

Fund raising at the Coast had been successful and, with the money which over the years had accumulated for Mombasa, plus the £3,000 from the Education Department, it was possible to go ahead with the building. It will be remembered that a plot of land on the corner of Cliff Avenue had been allocated to the Association in 1924. The Hostel Foundation Stone was therefore laid which reads: "This Foundation Stone was laid by Lady Baden Powell on the 14th February 1950." This was exactly 38 years to the day that the Association started in Kenya. There is no means of knowing when the hostel opened, probably about August 1950.

In 1951 Maendeleo ya Wanawake was founded. This was a Government backed community development movement formed to accelerate the progress of African women. Maendeleo was very popular and grew rapidly.

Early in the year, Mrs Montgomery must have written again to Mrs French asking for an experienced staff member, for there is a copy of the reply in the Geneva archives which says "The Association could only look for outside support for work which was set to meet the needs of all women and girls." This seems rather a strange response to poor Betty Montgomery, who for years had been striving to do just that. Undaunted, in March the President sent another hand written letter to Mrs. French. She said that the A.G.M. was to be held the following Monday and that although she had been pressed to continue as President she felt that she had held the office for too long. It would seem that she had indeed been Nairobi Branch President for four or five years. Mrs Claude Anderson, wife of the Managing Director of the East African Standard, was now Vice-President. Doreen had resigned from the Committee as she was too busy to attend meetings. Betty Montgomery seemed disappointed about this for she continues "…there can be no new endeavours with the present set up". We cannot but feel sorry for her, she sounds so frustrated. She had consulted the Government authorities and representatives of the Municipality and several other bodies about the possibility of starting work with African women and it was generally agreed that this was urgently needed, but she says "No one seems to have the time nor do we know how to begin. We need a staff member from World's Headquarters to come and do the spade work. I still wish someone like Miss Mills could come out and organise other YWCA work". She reported that both the Nairobi and Mombasa hostels were going very well and that her Committee was strong and enthusiastic. The Nairobi Branch Secretary was a Miss Flower who was due to leave in August and would be replaced by Miss Helen Plumpton who had worked in girls' clubs, presumably in England. The President concluded this long letter "I live in great hopes of new activities with Miss Plumpton's aid".

This cri de coeur had some effect for, in January 1952 Mrs French wrote to the Nairobi Committee saying that the British Association would be willing to recruit a professional worker, to provide the money for her passage and half the first year's salary, on condition that Nairobi found the additional finance and agreed "...to broaden their programme to include all races." Instead of enthusiastically accepting this wonderful offer, the Committee hesitated and no doubt there was much argument and discussion, for on 20th February, Branch Secretary Helen Plumpton wrote saying that the Annual General Meeting would be taking place in March when Mrs Montgomery would be retiring as President and would be replaced by Mrs Claude Anderson. It would seem that the new President was the daughter-in-law of one of the founder members mentioned in 1912. Helen Plumpton's letter continued by stating that a new Constitution had been drafted. Mrs Anderson would be going to London H.Q. after the A.G.M. and would be taking a copy for the O.F.D. Committee to study. Miss Plumpton explained that the Committee wanted to be sure that they "...were working on a sound basis, before developing or expanding the work." There is no further correspondence until the following January, so it is not possible to know what the O.F.D. thought of the Constitution. It is apparent that the Nairobi Committee did not take up the splendid offer suggested by Mrs French, which must have been a great disappointment for the retiring President. Of course, the Committee's hesitation may have been partly due to the fact that the Emergency was creating great difficulties at that time. However, a Nairobi minute records that a letter was received from World's H.Q. Geneva asking if work with African women could not be started. An ad hoc Committee was therefore set up to consider what, if anything, could be done.

New factories were opening up in Nairobi and African girls were leaving their villages to seek work in the City. The C. P. K. book "Rabai to Mumias" records that "...as late as the 1950s the mission house at Pumwani, Nairobi, made a room available for working girls who had not managed to find decent accommodation." There can be little doubt that the time was overdue for the YWCA to provide this service.

At long last the building of All Saints, the Cathedral of the Highlands, was complete and on 21st March 1952, it was consecrated by Bishop Crabbe.

Towards Integration — 1953

During the year Frank Boedeker suddenly died leaving Doreen a widow after only seven years. Miss Plumpton appears to have resigned in December and Doreen was asked if she would take over from her.

By January 1953 Doreen Boedeker was Branch Secretary and Hostel Warden. Being a trained YWCA worker, she longed for the day when the Nairobi Association would become a true YWCA and work with women of all races. She tells how she would sit at her Reception Desk, which in those days overlooked a cornfield, on which now stand Alico (American Life Insurance Company), Minet ICDC, Watumishi wa Wote Co-operative House, Shelter Afrique House and other high-rise buildings, and watch Kikuyu women walking through the maize, burdened with loads strapped round their heads and often a baby curled up in towels on their backs, and would say to herself "One day they, or perhaps their babies, will be YWCA members."

Doreen had been asked by the Committee to deal with all correspondence with World's YWCA. She sent a resumé of the work being done by the Association to World's H.Q. explaining that the Mau Mau Emergency had hindered plans for development. She informed them that an ad hoc committee had been set up to discuss the need for an African girls' hostel. She reported that a request for Club Work had been received from as far away as Kakamega.

In February Mrs French wrote to the Nairobi President telling her that Mrs. Calkin, a member of World's Executive Committee would be visiting Nairobi. There is no information about this visit but in May, presumably after Mrs. Calkin had left, Mrs Anderson wrote to Mrs French saying that because of the Emergency, she dared not leave her farm in the evening and that she hoped Mrs Calkin would visit Kenya again in happier times.

Mrs Anderson also wrote to Marguerite Spiers, International Secretary of the British YWCA asking that the appointment of a General Secretary be postponed for the time being.

The next available information comes from a letter to Janet Thomson, Mutual Service Secretary, World's YWCA. On 12th May 1953, Doreen wrote to her saying that a successful A.G.M. had taken place in April. Quoting from the President's Report she said the Emergency had brought anxieties and problems to both committee and staff. The Hostel was full with 70 Residents between the age of 16 and 25, fees varying from £10 to £14 per month; an extension was very necessary. The Residents' Committee was functioning well and Club activities within the Hostel were fencing, Scottish dancing, table tennis and a music circle; the tennis courts were always in great demand. There had been two visitors from U.K., Miss Spiers and Miss Pilkington; Miss Sue Stille had visited from the YWCA Uganda. The report continued by saying that it was hoped to establish a Colony Council with a Secretary who would develop work among all races. Doreen added a personal note to this letter "...I believe that there is now a real interest in the YWCA as a World-Wide Association and not just as a Hostel, in Kenya."

Miss Lilace Barnes, President World's YWCA visited Kenya in May and apparently stayed with Mrs Anderson from 23rd-26th. In June Mrs Anderson wrote to Helen Roberts, World's General Secretary, saying that the visit had been "a great Joy." She added that she hoped an experienced staff member from either Britain or Canada would soon be seconded to Nairobi so that club activities could be developed from Windsor House Hostel.

This is the year that the Right Reverend Leonard Beecher became Bishop of Mombasa and he and his wife began to take a personal interest in the development of the YWCA. On the 15th of June, the Rev. W. Scott-Dickson, General Secretary C.C.K. wrote to the World's President, whom no doubt he had met during her recent visit, saying that he believed that the present YWCA Committee had become aware of the needs in Kenya. He did not think, however, that the time had come for a General Secretary. He considered the urgent requirement was for a Programme Secretary "...to extend the work out from Windsor House into the African and Asian sections of the City." He recommended that a General Secretary should be appointed at a later date. It is indeed curious that the idea was to work from Windsor House, situated in what was at that time, an entirely European area.

The only Minutes available are those of the Hostel Management Committee and Doreen was requested to write to London H.Q. and ask for a Programme Secretary to organise multi-racial work from Windsor House. London replied that the letter had been forwarded to World's YWCA in Geneva, for although the British Association could lend a staff member, they could not provide any money.

Before long World's YWCA responded accepting the offer of Mary Suthren from Great Britain and saying that through their Mutual Service Fund the YWCA of Canada had agreed to be responsible for all expenses for three years.

In October 1954 Mary Suthren flew from London to Geneva to be given her brief. World YMCA owned a very fine residence in Geneva, John Mott House, and World's YWCA rented part of the building for their H.Q. It was situated in a beautiful position overlooking the lake. Mary's brief was "To promote work with women and girls of all races." She could hardly have been sent to Kenya at a more difficult time, for the Emergency was at its height between 1953 and 1956.

When Mary met the Committee in Nairobi, she soon realised that some members were not interested in her multi-racial approach. She remembers being given wonderful encouragement and guidance by the Bishop's wife, Glady's Beecher, née Leakey, who was Vice-President. Elizabeth Bostock, wife of Archdeacon Peter Bostock, Mrs Carol MacCrae and several others were very supportive. Doreen Boedeker was of course most welcoming, as she began to see her dream coming true.

Towards Integration — 1954

Mary's accommodation was a small bedroom on the ground floor by the Reception and she had to share Doreen's office. According to Mary, the rope ladders hanging from the verandah were being misused. She remembers hearing residents climbing down after the Hostel had closed at night and returning in the small hours! Soon Windsor House Committee decided to take a risk and have the ladders removed; fortunately no fire occurred. When a new west wing was being considered, a good fire escape was included in the plans.

Mary was a Methodist, and there being in those days no church of that denomination in Nairobi, she joined the congregation of St. Andrew's Presbyterian Church and soon became friendly with Mrs. Elizabeth Jacobs, an Asian woman from Kerala, South India, a member of the ancient Syrian Orthodox Church, and through her, she had an introduction to the Indian Girls' High School.

Into the New Kenya
1955-1965

1955. Colony Council instituted.
First Africans enrolled as Full Members in Nairobi and Mombasa

This year was indeed a watershed for the Kenya Association.

On 20th January, a Round Table conference was convened, chaired by Rt. Revd. Leonard Beecher, Bishop of Mombasa. The purpose of the meeting was to discuss the formation of a Colony Council. The Bishop referred to the good work started at Bishopsbourne in 1913. Mr. Morrison, General Secretary of the C.C.K., said that he had seen multi-racial work in Cairo and envisaged the same possibility in Nairobi. Jean Wanjiru, represented the Girl Guides and spoke of the needs of African girls in the City; this was endorsed by Helen Chania. Church leaders present stressed the urgency of setting up club work with African women in Nairobi. The following proposition was agreed: "We as a Round Table Conference, would like to give wholehearted support to the plans put forward today for the development and expansion of the YWCA in Kenya and agree to the formation of a Colony Council." A week later on 28th January, another important meeting took place chaired by Vice-President Mrs Beecher. Three propositions were presented and approved:

1. that a Colony President be elected.
2. that four Trustees be appointed.
3. that District Representatives from Nairobi, Mombasa, Rift Valley, and Central Province become the Colony Council be appointed.

It was resolved that these three proposals should be sent to London for the approval of World's Council which would be meeting there in September. Mrs Claude Anderson was still President of the Nairobi Branch. Unfortunately there is no way of finding out why she did not chair this meeting or why the Report, which was regarded as the new Constitution, was sent to London and not to Geneva.

With the invaluable help of the Bishop and his wife, and through contacts with other Church leaders and various social workers, Mary Suthren started a group for African women early in the year. Being the Emergency period, there were numerous restrictions which slowed down her progress, but the first African group met weekly, always having to change its venue because of the Emergency regulations. Sometimes they met at Bahati, on other occasions at Pumwani, Bondeni or Ofafa. Mrs Hannah Rubia was elected the first Chairman. She is mentioned frequently in this history and some years later was to become National Patron.

Into the New Kenya — 1955

The Trustees met with the Executive and the Hostel Management Committees on 10th March and plans for the extension to Windsor House were discussed. It was decided that the new wing should have 45 beds. The two wooden huts erected in 1943, known as the "pre-fabs" were being used by Windsor House for extra accommodation. The reader will remember that Jackie Taffs had promised that the Kenya Association would inherit all property belonging to the War Services. A clause regarding the appointment of a General Secretary for Kenya was added to the draft Constitution and copies were sent to all Full Members in the country, at that time numbering only thirty. A request had been received for a hostel in Nakuru. Mrs Nicholson, President Mombasa Branch, never reached the meeting as her train was derailed. Fortunately she returned to Mombasa safely. The Bishop asked the Executive for powers to be given to the Trustees to take any necessary action with regard to grants, loans and properties. This was granted.

The four Trustees were certainly kept busy, for, on 25th March they met again with the Executive Committee and at this meeting it was reported that the E.A.W.L. had agreed to open a hostel in Nakuru. This was just as well, for the YWCA was not at this juncture increasing work with Europeans; multi-racial work was now the agenda. The meeting decided that the City Council's African Affairs Officer should be invited to join the Executive Committee. A minute records that "Windsor House servants quarters was discussed." This is an important minute because the stone quarters built in 1941 were situated exactly where the Bishop anticipated the new lower income hostel should be sited. Obviously the Trustees were thinking ahead. It was noted that Lady O'Connor, wife of the President of the Court of Appeal, had agreed to serve on the Hostel Committee. Mrs Boedeker was instructed to write and ask her if she would be willing to become the first Colony President. Mary Suthren reported that she had rented the war-time Toc H Hut in Whitehouse Road at a rent of Sh. 27.50 a week. Since 1946, the Hut had been used by the Scouts. This was to be the meeting place for all African and multi-racial activities. The idea of Windsor House being used for this purpose seemed to have been forgotten. Preparing the Hut was the first multi-racial project undertaken by the Association. Several Windsor House residents assisted with the decorating and painting and members of the African group made the curtains. The official opening was planned for 14th April.

On 29th March 1955 Windsor House held its A.G.M., presumably chaired by Mrs Anderson. During the meeting, the new concept of an Executive Council was explained and agreed. Tea followed and at 6 p.m the Executive Committee of the Colony Council, chaired by Lady O'Connor, met for the first time. The main item on the agenda was to receive a report from the ad hoc Committee which had been looking into the possibility of setting up a hostel for African girls. The recommendations were as follows;-

a. The hostel should be for educated African girls working in the City.

b. It was not to be sited in the Locations but near where the girls were employed.
c. It should be near a church; Cathedral Hill might be a possibility.
d. A European warden should be in charge for the first few years.
e. The suggested plan was for a clubroom on the ground floor with accommodation for fifty girls above.

Mary Suthren was told to write to the City Council, and ask for a site, either on Cathedral Hill or on Whitehouse Road, to be allocated to the YWCA, and invite the Mayor to meet the Trustees.

Early in the year Mary had visited the Hostel in Mombasa. As in Nairobi, all the residents were European and Mary did not feel very welcome. The President of the Mombasa Committee, however, was interested in what Mary was trying to do and invited her to move from the Hostel and stay with her and her husband, Commander Nicholson; she also arranged for Mary to meet some of the leading African women at the Coast.

On World Membership day, 27th April, the first multi-racial Enrolment Service was held. Hannah Rubia, Phoebe Asiyo, Muthoni Likimani, Mary Radia, Beth James and Perpetua Kaigwa, all members of the newly formed African group, together with several Windsor House residents and some Asians, including girls from the High School, were enrolled.

There is a letter in World's YWCA files from Mary dated 28th June 1955 telling Janet Thomson that Mrs. Anderson had resigned as President Nairobi Branch because she wished to give more time to the E.A.W.L. She seems to have been an able President. She had entertained the World President and other YWCA guests and it was she who had taken the draft of the first revised Constitution to H.Q. in London in 1952. There was not to be a Nairobi Branch as such, for many years to come; the capital city was needed financially and socially as a focal point for developing a national movement.

The Colony Executive Committee met on 4th July when a letter was read from Janet Thomson reminding the Association that since 1918 it had been a "Corresponding Member" of the World Movement. The Association was invited to send two representatives to World's Council and Anne Ellis was elected to be a delegate together with Emma Njonjo who was studying in U.K. The Bishop reported, with regret, that there had been no progress with regard to either a site for an African hostel or to a Government grant; plans for the Windsor House extension were complete but no building could commence until funds were available. The Meeting decided that the first meeting of the Kenya Colony Council should be arranged to coincide with the E.A.W.L. A.G.M. as many women would be interested in attending both.

A second Enrolment took place in the Hut on 13th July when eight Africans and four Europeans (one being Jillian Cossar) became full members. Miss Winifred Galbraith, Religious Education Secretary World's YWCA happened to

Into the New Kenya — 1955

be visiting Kenya and conducted the Service. Mrs Margaret Hathaway, World's YWCA Advisory Secretary to Southern Africa was passing through Nairobi at the time and she joined in the celebrations which culminated with a "fork" supper.

By September, Anne Ellis had been briefed by Mary and Doreen and was prepared to leave for World's Council; this was the first time that Kenya had been able to send a delegate. It will be remembered that the Nairobi Branch had been invited to attend a World's Conference in Budapest in 1928.

1955 was the Centenary year of the YWCA, which had been founded in London. World's Council, therefore, met there and it was then that Isabel Catto of the British Association was elected World President. The Centenary celebrations culminated with a Service of Thanksgiving in St. Paul's Cathedral in London and the Kenya Association organised a service in All Saints' Cathedral in Nairobi which took place at exactly the same time, using the same Service sheets. At this World Council meeting it was decided that Geneva H.Q. would no longer be referred to as World's but World YWCA.

At the meeting of the Trustees held jointly with the Executive and Hostel Committees on the 15th September, the Bishop said that £30,000 would be required, either by grant or loan, to build the new wing for Windsor House. He explained that it had become clear that the matter could not be discussed at Government level if the project was treated on a racial basis. He insisted that the proposed buildings must be part of a total YWCA project on a long term plan. He assured the Executive that the Trustees would give their full support to the building of the West wing extension, if it were built at the same time as a lower income hostel which could be sited 70 yards to the south of Windsor House. He estimated that the cost of the new hostel would be approximately £15,000.

A meeting in October of the Trustees with the Executive and Hostel Committees was attended by the Asst. Secretary for Local Government. A member of the Hostel Committee asked about the clause in the Deeds that the YWCA plot was for Europeans only. The Bishop assured them that this could easily be rectified. Another member asked what guarantee there was that if the Hostel Committee gave permission for the lower income hostel to be built alongside Windsor House that the new west wing would be built also. The Bishop said that the Trustees would make it a condition that both were built at the same time. He was then asked what chance there was of a Government grant for the west wing extension, to which he replied "very little", but he assured the Hostel Committee that the scheme had the full support of the Trustees.

Mary returned to Mombasa in November and enrolled the first African women at the Coast including Mary Omolo and Maggie Gona, both subsequently to become National Chairmen, also Grace John, Ida Mbotela, Mrs Watts, Phoebe Ogenja, Nora Ogaye, and Mrs Maria Taylor whose maternal grandfather's life is of such international interest that his story must be included.

Maria was a founder member of the YWCA at Freretown, a village near Mombasa created by the Rev. W. Salter Price of the C.M.S. in 1875 to make homes for freed slaves. The place was very properly named after Sir Henry Bartle Frere the Special Commissioner appointed by the British Government to go to East Africa in 1872 to enquire into the traffic in slaves and who a year later, procured the signing, by the Sultan of Zanzibar, of a treaty abolishing the slave trade.

Matthew Wellington, Maria's grandfather whose real name was Susi Changwimbe, was the son and heir of a Yao Chief in what is now Malawi. In 1860 when he was about 15 he was sold by an envious uncle to Arab slave traders, who put him and other captured people in chains and marched them to the coast, a terrible and very dangerous journey of about 300 miles which, according to Susi, took "several moons". Those who survived were herded onto a dhow bound for Arabia via Zanzibar. Fortunately the dhow was captured by the Royal Navy, the slaves freed and taken to a settlement in India about 50 miles inland from Bombay which had been established by the C.M.S. for freed slaves. There, Susi became a Christian, was given the name Matthew Wellington, and trained to be a stone mason.

In India he met Dr. David Livingstone who suggested that Susi, now Matthew, should return to Africa with him; no doubt Doctor Livingstone realised that Mathew's knowledge of that continent, its customs and languages would be invaluable to him.

For seven years they travelled together exploring and preaching the Gospel and Matthew became Dr. Livingstone's trusted friend and faithful servant.

It was Matthew, who found the good Doctor when he died at Ilala in 1873. There were four other faithful Africans in the Doctor's service, and they wanted to bury their master immediately but Matthew knew that Doctor Livingstone's wish was that he should be taken to Bagamoyo, the port from which dhows sailed to and from Zanzibar. So after Matthew had cut out the heart and buried it, they set about preserving the body with salt. Then the five carried the body over 15 hundred miles to Bagamoyo, a journey which took them nine months.

Matthew and his companions accompanied Dr. Livingstone's body to England and were present in Westminster Abbey for the official burial in April 1874.

Matthew Wellington sailed back to Africa and was given a plot of land by the C.M.S. at Kilindini Migobani, near Mombasa, where he became a valuable assistant to the Rev. Salter Price.

Matthew married, and one of his daughters, Florence Ruth, became the wife of an engineer, a descendant of a freed slave from Barbados, who was working on the construction of the Kenya/Uganda Railway. His name was Joseph Christopher Douglas and they were married at Emmanuel Church, Kisauni, which had been completed in 1889.

Into the New Kenya — 1955

YWCA members at the Asian Girls' High School, Nairobi

In 1910 their daughter Maria was born, and when she was twenty five she became Mrs Taylor. Her famous grandfather retired with pensions from the British Government and the C.M.S. Every month Maria accompanied him into Mombasa to collect his pensions until the time of his death at the age of ninety in 1935.

The Uganda YWCA invited Kenya to send a representative to Kampala during the annual YM/YW Week of Prayer and World Fellowship. Writing in the autumn edition of "The Blue Triangle", the magazine of the British Association, Mary explained that since the Emergency Regulations were in force no Kikuyu would be permitted to travel. Fortunately, a Luo member had been chosen, Mrs Damaris Ayodo. The article reads "Very few of these girls have travelled at all, so you can imagine the thrill. She will be all night on the train, but I doubt if she will sleep! We are having various efforts for the train fare, which needs some finding".

During November, Mary was able to start groups in Machakos Girls' High School and in the African Girls' High School thus creating important members for the future.

Towards the end of the year, Geneva files stated that the C.C.K. asked the YWCA to develop programme work among women and girls in the new community centres and African locations of Nairobi.

Late in November, the Hostel Committee wrote to the Colony President saying that they were very disappointed when the Bishop had said that the the £30,000 loan could not be obtained unless they gave permission for the lower income hostel to be built "on their site" a proposal which they felt "would be a pity". A joint meeting of the Executive and Hostel Committee was therefore called on 2nd

Inter-racial netball match

December which the President asked the Bishop to attend. He explained that the National Bank of India was prepared to negotiate the loan of £30,000 on condition that all assets, including the £15,000 now promised for the lower income hostel, were mortgaged. If Windsor House Committee decided not to let their site be used, the new hostel could not be built, thus the mortgage value would be reduced by £15,000 and although the loan of £30,000 might still be available, the interest rate would be considerably increased. The Hostel Committee withdrew to another room to discuss the situation. On returning they put forward the following Resolution "On the understanding that the African Hostel has its own Board of Management and Finance Committee, Windsor House Committee gives approval for its erection on their site and asks the Trustees to continue negotiating for a loan of £30,000 using the total site and all assets, as security for the mortgage". It is interesting to note that whereas the Trustees refer to the building as the "Lower Income Hostel" meaning for all races, Windsor House Committee is convinced that it will be occupied entirely by Africans!

Before the end of this momentous year, Geneva files record that an inter-racial netball match was played on a pitch lent by a local school — we don't know who won!

Into the New Kenya — 1956

1956. Bahati Hostel opens for African girls. YWCAs formed in Kisumu, Kakamega and Meru. Work begins in Kikuyu villages

The first A.G.M. of the Colony Council took place at Windsor House on 2nd February, 1956. The President, Lady O'Connor, was in the chair. Council agreed that the appointment of a Colony Secretary should be considered in the near future.

Commenting on the discussion which had taken place during 1954 and 1955 about the need to set up an inexpensive hostel for African girls, it was stated that no land for this purpose had been granted. The Colony Council, therefore, decided to approach the Mayor, Alderman I. Somen, and ask him if there was any possibility of renting some suitable accommodation. This resulted in ten old police houses at Bahati being made available by the City Council who agreed to let these to the YWCA at the usual Council rent. Bahati was near the Industrial Area where many girls were working in factories. This compound consisted of ten single storied rooms, each with its own front door on to a verandah. At the far end between the two rows of rooms, there was a communal ablution block with showers and laundry facilities. A high barbed wire fence enclosed the site and the Warden lived in the house nearest the gate. The room on the opposite side of the gate was turned into a Common Room with electric light, and books, magazines and games were kept there. Every evening, some educational, recreational or social programme was organised and greatly appreciated. The residents paid Shs.16 a month for a three bedded room, Shs.25 for a twin bedded room and Shs.42 if they required a room to themselves. The girls had to provide their own furniture, bedding, oil lamps for lighting, and charcoal or oil stoves for cooking their food which took place on their verandahs. Most of the residents

The opening of the Bahati Hostel in April 1956

went home to their villages at weekends, returning by bus on Sunday night with sufficient food from their parents' shambas to last them the week. On 1st February Mrs Coleen Partridge was appointed warden on a two year contract and Jillian Cossor, a Full Member, offered to be the Honorary Treasurer.

On March 27th Mary Suthren attended the A.G.M. of the Mombasa Branch, at which fifty Europeans were present. Mrs Greenwood was elected President. Mary received an invitation from Mrs Mary Omolo to visit her the following morning to meet the Africans who had been enrolled as Full Members the previous November. This led to the establishment of the first African Branch in Mombasa. Meetings were held regularly in Mrs Omolo's house; later she formed a branch in Tudor. Mary Suthren had been told by Bishop Beecher that she should try to meet Miss E. B. M. Lloyd, Municipal Welfare Officer, Mombasa. Mary contacted her and this resulted in Miss Lloyd becoming a very helpful member.

A joint meeting of the Windsor House Hostel Committee and the Trustees was held in April, when the means of funding the proposed building projects in Nairobi were established. The £30,000 needed for the Windsor House extension would be obtained by two loans:

Short term loan from National Bank of India £15,000
City Council loan (repayable in 20 years) £15,000
(Both being negotiated by the Trustees.)

The building of the lower income hostel was to be funded as follows:
Promise of Local Government grant £ 8,000
Already banked towards this project £10,120

This included the grants from the War Memorial Committee and from the African Trust Fund.

It was decided that a new Committee be formed to take responsibility for the lower income hostel. The Bishop and Mrs Beecher suggested that some training scheme for African women and girls might be set up in the new hostel.

Unfortunately the stone built servants' quarters erected in 1941 had to be demolished; this of course was necessary as they were situated on the site where the lower income hostel was to be built. Fortunately more land had been acquired in 1939 and it was on the southern boundary of this latest plot that the new quarters were built at the cost of £3,000.

In August the Windsor House Committee wrote to the City Council and requested that the title deeds of the site be altered to permit the building of accommodation for African residents.

The Minutes record that a Mrs Edith Mate of Embu who had recently completed a Tropical Community Development Course given by Marjorie Stewart at YWCA Headquarters, London, had now returned to Kenya and was hoping to form a YWCA group in Embu.

Into the New Kenya — 1956

In a letter to Mary dated June 8th, Janet Thomson, writing from Geneva says "It is most encouraging that during the first half of your first term you have been able to extend the membership and expand the programmes so that the Kenya YWCA is recognised as an inter-racial fellowship." It was probably in this letter that Janet said she hoped to be in Kenya in August, for a note in Geneva files states that she, together with Isabel Catto, World President, had a meeting with Bishop Beecher in Nairobi. Apparently Isabel had been visiting Associations in the Far East and was due to fly back to London from India via Cairo. But rumours about the impending Suez crisis were rife in Delhi and she was advised to return by East Africa. This meant that she paid a short, unexpected but very welcome visit to Nairobi in August and it was probably then that she was asked to return in December to lay the foundation stones for the new buildings.

The YWCA still had no transport. Mary accepted lifts from anyone who had room for her in their car, or she travelled by train or bus. Early in the year 1956, she and a very loyal volunteer worker Mrs. Evie McIver, who was a Full Member of the YWCA, and wife of a YMCA staff member, had managed to organise a regular weekly lift to Banana Hill to assist Mrs. Lois Njeri who was running a Club for early school leavers. The programme was extended to include English, 1st Aid, Nutrition, Child Care and how to cook in a hay box, a method which was extremely useful to those rural women for it meant that when they returned after a day's work in their shambas, the family meal was ready. This was a very jolly group and the day always finished up with songs and games. Forty four years after it had been minuted that "dancing was outside the sphere of the Association" Mary was to discover that although dances were a regular feature of the Hostel programme, some European and most African Christians still considered it to be an unsuitable activity. Even tribal dancing was discouraged. Hearing that some liberal missionaries were getting away with Country Dancing, Mary decided to teach the Scottish Reels which the villagers greatly enjoyed. Part of her equipment was a wind-up portable gramophone and records and it was to this music that the village women happily danced.

Early in the year Mary was driven to Meru, where with the support of the Methodist Church and the help of Alice Nkloti, a YWCA group was formed.

During 1956 the International Club was founded. Meetings started after 4 p.m. so that working girls, some of whom were Windsor House residents, could get to the Whitehouse Road Hut direct from their offices. This club was the first of its kind in Kenya, enabling women of all races to meet together socially on a regular basis.

Mary also started what was to have been a Junior Girls' Club, but as their little brothers wanted to join, they were included. The members were mostly the children of European staff employed by the East African Railways and living in the vicinity of the Whitehouse Road Hut. Mary was disappointed that no African children were able to join, but in those days, none lived in that part of the city.

Kikuyu villagers learning Scottish reels

On 13th/14th October the first Full Members' Conference was held at Pumwani Community Centre by courtesy of the Rev. Charles Tett.

By now Mary had made contact with Church leaders in several villages. Whenever transport was available, she would visit Ngewa, Gathiga, Multyurwa, Kabete, Kiambu, Kiambaa and Kambui.

Money for the Building Fund was coming in slowly but thinking that by December loans and grants would be settled, the World President, Isabel Catto, who would be visiting YWCAs in Africa, had been invited to lay the foundation stones. Unfortunately insufficient money had been raised, and that is why there is a stone Bird Bath in the garden! This was hastily built, for Isabel to "unveil" signifying the first part of the new building programme. The inscription read "This plaque commemorates the visit of the Hon'ble Isabel Catto, World President YWCA, and marks the inauguration of the two new hostel building projects. December 3rd 1956." The Local Government grant of £8,000, promised by Nairobi Council towards the building of the lower income hostel, was received in December, just after she had left.

Into the New Kenya — 1957

It was decided in December to change the name from Windsor to Montgomery House as another building in Nairobi was called Windsor House. It will be remembered that Mrs Betty Montgomery had served on the Committee for many years, first when she was Mrs Galton-Fenzi. The name was never generally accepted, however, and it was the new wing which became Montgomery House.

Doreen Boedeker in October asked to be relieved of her post by the end of the year. Her resignation was received with much regret. She had been with the Nairobi YWCA either as staff or volunteer, for 12 years. London H.Q. was asked to send a replacement.

In December, Mary travelled to Kisumu where with the help of Isabel Apindi and Mary Omolo's sister, a YWCA group was founded. Isabel was the daughter of a great Luo churchman, The Reverend Canon Ezekiel Apindi, famous for his hospitality. It was said that he even provided new toothbrushes for his overnight guests. From Kisumu Mary went to Kakamega where the Society of Friends welcomed her and helped in the formation of a YWCA group. It will be remembered that a request for assistance with club work had been received from Kakamega as long ago as 1953.

1957. Volunteers start educational classes for YWCA members at the Coast. YMCA set up YM/YW clubs in Kiambu villages.

There is a memo in the World YWCA files dated January 1957 which reads "Until now women of Kenya have had little or no opportunity of belonging to an International Fellowship. The YWCA is eager to offer this kind of experience during these crucial years." Mary's International Club had been started for this very purpose.

In January, Mrs. Gwyneth Jackson arrived from London to become Director of what was still an entirely European hostel. Janet Thomson had written to her from Geneva in October 1956 saying that "The Kenya Association must move forward adventurously and confidently in building up multiracial work". Windsor House was full, with a waiting list and making a good profit. The standard of food and service continued to be high and it was regarded as good value for money. The best single rooms cost Shs.500 per month and shared rooms Shs.320 and Shs.440: this, of course, included an excellent full board. Nothing can be found in the Minutes about the appointment of Mrs. E. Middleton the Assistant Warden, known as "Mid" but Mary Suthren remembers that she arrived during 1957.

The Executive Committee of the Colony Council met on 22nd January and they set out membership fees as follows:

Life Membership	Shs.100
Normal Membership	Shs.7.50 per year
Plus Capitation Fee of	Shs.2.50

By March, it was time to consider Mary Suthren's first long leave as her three year contract would be terminating in September. So determined were the Executive Committee that Mary should be invited to serve a second term that they approached World H.Q. Geneva, the Department of Education Kenya and the C.C.K. asking for funds to cover her salary and expenses for the next three years. But time was running out and still there were no firm promises. To make sure that Mary did return, members of the Executive Committee personally guaranteed sufficient money for her air passage back to Kenya, together with salary and expenses for one year.

There is no record of an A.G.M. for 1957 but it is likely that it was held before Lady O'Connor went on leave to England. No doubt she would have been asked to discuss with the British Association the possibility of sending a General Secretary to Kenya. It was Lady O'Connor who represented the Kenya Association at the British Tri-annual Conference held on the Isle of Man.

Vera Harley, who was on the YWCA staff in London remembers her at that Conference, little thinking that, in the not too distant future, they would be working closely together.

During 1957, the YMCA started joint YM/YW clubs in several Kikuyu villages. Mary was not aware of this project. When she did hear about it, she was concerned because she felt that these village people were being misinformed if they were being told that there was a YM/YW World Organisation. Real commitment could only be achieved, she thought, if the men and women were encouraged to join their appropriate Associations, and then decided which part of their programmes should be held jointly.

A Full Members' conference was held on 20th/21st July at the CMS Community Centre at Pumwani. Over 20 members of all three races attended. Maggie Gona represented Mombasa and was the only African present who did not live in Nairobi. As the Hostel was still limited to Europeans, Mrs Likimani, a Nairobi member, offered Maggie hospitality.

Bahati Hostel was running successfully. Coleen Partridge, was not only Hostel Warden and Club Organiser but had set up YWCA groups in Ofafa, Dunman Road, Bondini, Starehe and was preparing to start work in Pumwani, Kaloleni and Mbotela. It was essential that Colleen took annual leave but this was not easy to arrange as Mary, being the sole member of staff, was not available to stay at Bahati for more than a week-end. Marjorie King, a Full Member, who was on the staff of the C.M.S. Bookshop, came to the rescue. Twice she nobly agreed to spend every evening and night at the Hostel so that Colleen could take two weeks leave, once over Christmas 1956 and another fortnight early in 1958. Marjorie remembers Bahati Residents being incredulous when it was explained to them that she had a full time job and was covering for their Warden's holiday on a voluntary basis.

Into the New Kenya — 1958

A donation of Shs.2725 was received from the Kenya Coffee Association; this was equally divided between the Colony Council fund, the European hostel extension and the Bahati Hostel.

The Mombasa Hostel was going well and had made a good profit. Educational work at the Coast was beginning under the volunteer leadership of Mrs Kitty Hall, a Canadian, who, before her marriage, as Kitty Pepler, had worked for World YWCA in India and Egypt. Her team of voluntary helpers included Barbara Greenwood, Helen Haylett and Katy Vile among others. Classes were being planned for early school leavers as well as for women in Mombasa, Tudor, Buxton and Freretown.

Working plans for the new lower income hostel and for the new wing to Windsor House were drawn and accepted and building was due to begin simultaneously in the New Year. It was very sad that several magnificent Jacaranda trees with their beautiful bluebell-like blossom had to be cut down. These had to go before the foundations of the new wing could be laid. Fortunately a few were saved.

The population of Nairobi was now 230,000 comprising 131,000 Africans, 77,000 Asians and 22,000 Europeans. Six African elected members took their seats in the House of Representatives; later in the year African Representation increased to fourteen. 1957 will be remembered as the year when Nairobi's beautiful City Hall was opened.

1958. Beecher House and new wing to Windsor House built.

Mary returned from leave on 2nd January 1958 to find that Executive had moved her into a much better room at the end of the Annex. This was large enough to serve as a bed sitting-room and office. She also found that British Inter-church Aid (which was to become Christian Aid) had agreed to support her for three years with sufficient funds to buy a car for the Association, and on 8th April a Morris Station wagon, KFX 201, was purchased. This made Mary's life much easier. She was now able to revisit Meru and go regularly not only to see the High School Y-teens at Kikuyu and Machakos, but also village groups at Gathiawa, Ngewa, and to Banana Hill, where Lois Koinange was proving to be a very responsible leader. Singers, the Sewing Machine Company, were very helpful, lending one of their staff, Helen Chania, to go to the villages with Mary to teach dressmaking.

The YWCA was given a warm welcome at the new Machakos Teacher Training College, the first teacher training institution for African women run by the Government of Kenya. Hitherto such colleges had been the responsibility of various missionary societies. The first Principal, Alison Shrubsole, was sent out by the Colonial Office in 1957. She tells how at the age of 33 and with no African experience, she was mildly surprised to find that the College buildings, whose plans she had approved in London, were not even begun; there was just a patch of recently cleared bush and an array of building materials. So she literally camped

The West-wing extension to Windsor House

out in a tent while the post and panel buildings were erected. Gathering staff and students, furnishing and equipping the college, and designing the curriculum gave her a busy six months before the College opened. Those early days were enlivened, she recalls, by the number of snakes disturbed when the trees and scrub had been cleared prior to the commencement of building. One evening the telephone rang in the shed which was her office and to her dismay there was a largish snake between the door and the phone. As she was wearing wellington boots, she decided to stand on the neck of the snake to take the call which was from the Director of Education. She wondered what he made of her reply that all was going well, except that she did not know how long it would take for the snake to die! The College opened in March and very soon an enthusiastic YWCA group was operating.

The Colony A.G.M. was held on 6th February 1958 and it was reported that World YWCA was advertising the post of General Secretary, Kenya.

At the March Executive, a letter was read from Geneva stating that the candidate recommended by Great Britain, namely Vera Harley, had applied for the post of General Secretary.

The April minutes report that the Technical College Committee would not grant permission for the entrance to the lower-income hostel to be on "their"

Into the New Kenya — 1958

road! This must have caused great consternation amongst the Hostel Committee because they were still opposed to the idea of African girls, who would be living in the new hostel, using "their" entrance.

In May, Janet Thomson arrived from Geneva and the appointment of a General Secretary was discussed. It was decided that the post should be offered to Vera Harley on a three year contract. Her salary would start at £475 per annum, rising to £600, plus an annual food allowance of £150. Free accommodation and transport would be provided. Referring to the World Council meeting which was to be held in Mexico in September 1959, Janet recommended that the Kenya Association should be upgraded from being a "Corresponding" member, to affiliation under "Category C." From Nairobi Janet wrote to World General Secretary, Elizabeth Palmer, saying that she had attended the Windsor House Committee meeting when it had been said "As a Christian Movement we cannot but be multi-racial here". Janet, no doubt, assumed that in future Windsor House would be open to all races, but sadly this did not happen for some years. Janet's letter continued "Mary is doing a remarkable job. Here we are, having a new YWCA experience among rural folk and can really be a creative force in this great super-imposed experiment of villagisation." Villages were a new way of living for the land owning Kikuyu. Before the Emergency, they had lived in family homesteads which meant that as the family grew up and extended, so more mud and wattle houses with thatched roofs were built. In order to protect the population, the British Army had insisted on creating villages. It must be remembered that throughout Mau Mau, 11,000 Africans, mainly Kikuyu, were killed, against only 124 European and Asians.

World Office notified Vera Harley that her application had been accepted and on Janet's return, she visited London, met Vera and arranged how her journey to Kenya should be organised. Vera was to leave London on 25th August and fly to Geneva for her briefing and thence to Athens, to attend a World YWCA Youth Training Course. The delegate from New Zealand was the young Erica Brodie; twenty years later she became World General Secretary. From Greece Vera was to fly to Kampala to see the YWCA work there and go on from Uganda by train to Nairobi where Mary would meet her.

As the train wound its way along the great Rift Valley Vera was enchanted by the beauty of the country and thrilled to see the pink rim caused by the masses of flamingos round the edge of Lake Nakuru. And never had she imagined the wonderful variety of the flowering trees and shrubs which adorned Nairobi not to mention the many species of brilliantly plumed birds. She was briefed in Geneva to create a national movement and to train Africans to run it. Vera pondered on this during her journey to Kenya. Much of what she felt is summed up in Anna Rice's "History of World YWCA" "Associations were being started in many lands on the lines of the countries from which the workers came, instead of on the lines

Beecher House — This picture was taken after the top floor had been added in 1969

especially adapted to the country for which they had been started". Vera could see how important it would be to set up groups in High Schools, Teacher Training Colleges and Universities so that an indigenous leadership could be created. She was encouraged, therefore, to find on arrival that Mary had groups already functioning in the two former, but not at that time, in the Technical College which was later to become the Royal College and in 1964, the University. As for a European type of Association being created in an African country, it was obvious to her that the YWCA in Kenya had been started by and for Europeans. It was Mary who had begun to break down racial barriers and to create a true YWCA.

Vera's salary and expenses for her first tour were made possible through a grant to World YWCA from British Inter-Church Aid, whose Director was Janet Lacey. Since Janet had been on the YWCA staff until 1946 before transferring to the YMCA, she was familiar with both Associations. It was considered that both

Into the New Kenya — 1958

Movements could help with the rehabilitation of young people in Kikuyu villages after the extremities of Mau Mau.

A bed-sit with bathroom and small kitchen had been rented for Vera from the British Council, situated in a cul-de-sac on the far side of the Arboretum. As she had no transport, it took her three quarters of an hour every morning to walk through the Arboretum to the YWCA. Not that she found this anything but enjoyable being amazed at the wonderful variety of beautiful trees. It was during one of these walks that she first saw what looked like a foot wide piece of black lace moving swiftly across the path! This of course was an army of safari ants. The hostel garden was another delight, bright with plants, many new to Vera. One she particularly liked was known as "Yesterday, Today and Tomorrow" the flowers being deep purple on the first day, mauve on the second and white on the third.

After a week or so, with no office, she asked Gwynneth Jackson to suggest to her Committee that a small space be found for her in Windsor House. The reply was that the Hostel Committee considered the work of the General Secretary to be quite separate from that of the Hostel and for that reason it would not be possible for her to have the use of any part of Windsor House.

The Committee structure on Vera's arrival was a Board of Trustees and a Finance Committee, both chaired by the Bishop; an Executive Committee and sub-committees for Windsor House Hostel, Programme and Membership, Lower-Income Hostel and African Estates. The Bishop discussed this structure with the General Secretary and mutually they agreed that the Executive Committee must be given the final responsibility. They therefore decided to recommend that the Finance Committee be discontinued for the time being and that the Executive should have the sub-title "General Purposes and Finance". The Board of Trustees would be given carefully defined Terms of Reference and the Colony President would be ex-officio on the Board of Trustees. The Bishop said that he would propose this to the National Council.

The two new buildings were growing rapidly. Vera asked Bishop Beecher why the lower income hostel had not been designed as an extension to Windsor House, so that existing well equipped kitchens could serve both hostels, Windsor House continuing with waiter service as long as this was required and the new hostel operating as selfservice. His answer was a sad one; he explained that the Windsor House Committee had not been willing to contemplate a multi-racial building. Had Vera read the Minutes of 1955, she need not have asked. They both knew, however, that soon opinions would change. As it happened, separate kitchens, although extravagant to run, enabled the Association to set up an educational project, details of which come later in this history.

Vera first met the the Executive Committee on 22nd September. The Hon. Mrs Jemima Gecaga, a member of Legislative Council, was the only non-European on the Committee. Sadly Coleen Partridge had given three month's notice, having been Warden of Bahati for almost three years. Running such a Hostel had been a real pioneering piece of work since it was the first residence for African girls in Nairobi. In her report, Coleen said that it took great courage for a girl to leave her village and come to work in Nairobi; many had never been to a city before and the change must have been traumatic. She considered that the YWCA's help was still vital. Coleen had won the confidence and respect of all the residents and indeed their affection and had helped them through a difficult transition period. The only other Minute of note was that Mrs. Hannah Rubia, Chairman of African Estates Committee, would be representing the Kenya Association at the W.C.C. Work Camp in Madagascar which would be lasting for three weeks.

By October, the new buildings in Nairobi were almost complete and discussion took place as to who should be appointed warden of the new lower income hostel. Mrs Beecher had recommended Edna Collins who was working with the C.M.S. in Maseno. Mary had previously met and talked with Edna about the new hostel and she too considered her to be a very suitable person. It was decided that Vera should take the train to Kisumu, where she happened to have friends with whom she could stay. This was a memorable journey because the train had no dining-car and at Londiani, everyone alighted including the engine driver and his mate, both Europeans, to be given an excellent meal. This was served in a wooden building while the engine took in sufficient water to produce the steam to pull the train up to the highlands around Molo. Whilst in Kisumu she met the YWCA group, chaired by Isabel Apindi, made some local church contacts and managed to find a lift to Maseno. Edna was expecting to be offered the post of Hostel Warden but Vera told her that before leaving England she had been invited to meet the Bishop and Mrs. Beecher, who were on leave in London. They had told her of the great need for vocational training explaining that the Anglican Church already had a school operating for boys in Nairobi, the Christian Industrial Training Centre. but as yet, nothing was available for girls. This idea had opened up a new vision to Vera as to how the current educational needs of African girls might, in some small way, be met by the YWCA. It was a vision shared by Edna who told Vera that she would only be willing to become Hostel Warden if it included a training for girls. She agreed to accept the very demanding and challenging post of Hostel Warden and Headmistress of a Vocational Training School to be set up in January; she promised to report for duty in mid-December.

Vera returned to Nairobi in time for the Christmas Market which was organised by Windsor House Committee and held in the Motor Mart, making a profit of Shs.1,600.

The Uganda YWCA had raised Shs.148.85 during the Week of Prayer and World Fellowship which they very generously donated to the Kenya Association.

Into the New Kenya — 1958

The N.G.S. felt that it was important that she should meet the Mombasa Committee as soon as possible and she was able to pay a short visit early in December. The first surprise was when she arrived at Nairobi railway station; all the city seemed to be there, people of all races shouting, hugging and waving. It reminded her of the send off when Atlantic liners sailed for America! The second surprise was seeing from the train a veritable zoo as the sun set over the Athi River plains. The very comfortable journey impressed her enormously, a delicious meal, excellent service and an extremely comfortable bed. But what intrigued her most was the slow and gradual descent from 5,500 ft. to sea level, the train taking twelve hours to snake its way down the 300 miles through ever changing scenery which could even be discerned in the brilliant moonlight. By dawn she found herself in what seemed to be another country with the temperature already in the eighties and the vegetation quite different from Nairobi with all the tropical fruit trees and shrubs. She had been told how beautiful the East African coast was and she was not disappointed.

Mrs Helen Haylett met the train and took Vera to the Hostel where she was made most welcome. Whilst being shown round by the Warden, Vera asked if there was any age limit for residents. The Warden laughed saying that had Miss Harley visited them a month earlier, she would have met a resident of over ninety. Vera asked what had happened to her. The Committee had decided that she could not stay any longer and she was now living in an hotel in Moshi; her name was Miss Tristram. "Not Tristy" said Vera. "Do you know her?" asked the Warden, astonished. Vera was mortified and asked for her address, for this was the remarkable Katherine Tristram, the first woman university graduate (she had a degree in Mathematics) to become a C.M.S. missionary. She was sent to Japan in 1888. After a life in the mission field she retired to Kenya where in 1942/3 she met Jean Begg. Tristy was then in her late seventies but J. B. assured her that she was not too old to be very useful and took her back to Cairo where Vera met her, a tiny figure dressed in khaki battle-dress with blue YWCA flashes. They became very fond of each other and she told Vera that her brother had been one of Queen Victoria's Private Secretaries. She was still helping with the War Service Work in Port Said when Vera sailed for home in January 1946. A few months after returning to Nairobi Vera was offered a lift to Moshi. Tristy was delighted to see her but not surprised as she had heard of Vera's appointment to Kenya. Within a year she had died. Had the Mombasa Committee known her background they would probably have allowed her to remain. It would indeed have been a privilege for the YWCA if Tristy had ended her days in one of their hostels.

The N.G.S. was taken to see Mombasa Cathedral, a beautiful Moorish style building set in an exotic tropical garden. Consecrated in 1905, it was the first Cathedral in East Africa. From the time it opened Christians of all races were welcomed, regular services being held in English and Swahili.

Rickshaws to Jets

She was disappointed not to meet any African members, her visit being so short but she was assured that this would be arranged during her next visit.

Vera gave her first report to the Executive in December. She was also Minutes Secretary so she was relieved when Lady O'Connor, who was in the chair, agreed that the Shs.200 she had in hand for a typewriter, could be used to engage a part-time typist at Shs.10 per hour. There were several typewriters available.

The N.G.S. told the Committee that since her arrival she had spent a great deal of time attending meetings and getting to know people; she was ex-officio on all YWCA Committees. Being one of the founder members of the Christian Council of Kenya, the Association was expected to be represented on several of its committees. She explained that in the past Mary had carried out this task. She had taken this over, thus releasing Mary to expand and consolidate her work in the townships and villages.

During her first few weeks Mary had taken the new N.G.S. to visit all nearby groups including the African Girls' High School. Vera had been able to visit Meru, the Rev. Elliot Kendall, Chairman of the Methodist Missionary Society in Kenya, kindly giving her a lift. During this safari Vera had looked forward to seeing Mount Kenya but it was shrouded in cloud all the time. She felt compensated, however, for not more than a hundred yards from the road were three giraffes, the graceful creatures watching the car pass before resuming their meal of succulent leaves high up on the trees. A little further on Vera spotted what looked like the skin of a deer hanging from a tree. It was of course a gerenuk, the only member of the buck family which stands on its hind legs to feed. Suddenly Elliot said "Quick windows up". A cloud of dust was rapidly approaching. This was the wake of a car. Being Vera's first experience of up-country roads, she was surprised to find on arriving at their destination, that she was covered with red dust. At Meru, she not only met Alice Nkloti's excellent group but also the members of the YM/YW of which the young D.O. Keith Foot, was a member, as indeed were most of the YWCA group. Before leaving she was taken by Chairman Elliot Kendall to meet the staff at the Methodist Mission, the Kenya HQ being in Meru, and she found them to be very interested in, and supportive of, the YWCA.

Reporting on her interview with Edna Collins in Maseno, the N.G.S. told Executive about her meeting with the Bishop and Mrs. Beecher in London when they had explained how urgent it was to organise training for early school leavers. Vera said that she had therefore discussed with Edna the possibility of setting up a small school within the new Hostel; Edna had shown great interest in this idea. Executive agreed that, as only male servants were employed in European homes, except for children's nurses, perhaps the time had come to open up these opportunities for girls. The N.G.S. explained that this was not what was being proposed. The Committee no doubt, knew that there were many African girls who, after eight years schooling, had passed the Kenya African

Into the New Kenya — 1958

Preliminary Examination, known as K.A.P.E., and were therefore entitled to a place in High School or Teacher Training College but that there were insufficient places to accommodate them. The only option for these girls was to return to their villages, where they would have no access to books and before long, much of their education would be forgotten. This was not only a dreadful waste of money but of woman power. The proposed plan was to offer a course to twelve girls who had taken K.A.P.E. They would not be trained to become house servants but offered a broad curriculum and after two years could sit for accredited examinations and thus be fitted to take up a wide variety of occupations.

As yet there was no Education and Training Committee, so Executive asked one of its members, Mrs. Elizabeth Normand, whose husband was in the Ministry of Education and whom Vera had met at one of Marjorie Stewart's training courses at the YWCA in London, to assist in drawing up a curriculum.

The N.G.S. then proposed that funds be found with which to build a National Block comprising Conference Room and offices on the ground floor, with more offices and two staff flats above. She pointed out that building rates were still cheap in Nairobi being only Shs.34 per square foot. Lady O'Connor said that she had discussed this proposition with the Bishop as Chairman of the Trustees and they both considered that, if possible, this scheme should go ahead.

By mid-December both new buildings, the lower income hostel and the extension to Windsor House, were completed; the former was named Beecher House for obvious reasons and the extension became known as Montgomery House. Beecher House comprised a Warden's flat, reception office, cloakrooms, lounge and dining room and kitchen on the ground floor, and above two floors of single and double rooms, two dormitories, bath units and laundry facilities. Edna arrived, as promised in mid-December and moved into Beecher House. It was only then realised that the architects had been at fault in putting the two floors of bathroom units immediately above the warden's flat. They should, of course, have been sited over the kitchens where the noise at night would not have caused any inconvenience. Four years later, Vera was gratified to discover from the architect that the foundations of Beecher House had been laid to carry another storey if and when required. Montgomery House consisted of forty single rooms with wash basins, adequate bathroom and laundry facilities, a staff flat and a fire escape.

The Hostel rates were as follows:

Windsor House & Montgomery House
Single room with full board per month	Shs.500
Double	Shs.440
3-4 bedded	Shs.320

Beecher House
Single room with breakfast and dinner

(and full board at week-ends) per month	Shs.240
Shared room ditto	Shs.190

Residents living in the war-time wooden buildings known as the "pre-fabs" were moved into Montgomery House but those army huts still had an important role to play.

Very gradually, girls began to book in at Beecher House. By Christmas there were several European Kenya girls who were either doing secretarial, book-keeping or hairdressing courses, one African, one Anglo-Indian, one Goan, one Seychelloise, one white South African, one Armenian, one Italian and one White American.

By now the N.G.S. had left her cul-de-sac and was living temporarily with Mrs Judy Dods (née Violet MacDonnell), and her husband and family in Lavington and every morning they drove Vera to the YWCA. Judy is mentioned earlier in the History as having worked with Vera in Cairo in 1944 and as so often happens in the YWCA World family, they now caught up again.

It was about this time that Vera received an invitation to lunch with Sir Godfrey and Lady Rhodes, of whom she had never heard. Sir Godfrey told her that a letter had arrived from a mutual friend in New Zealand, Jean Begg, saying "One of my girls is working in Nairobi, so look after her!" It will be remembered that Lady Rhodes was President Nairobi Branch in the 1930s. They became very good friends of Vera's.

The school year in Kenya terminated in December, so it was realised that no time must be wasted if twelve girls were to to start at the YWCA School in January. Through Mary's contacts and the girls in the YM/YW groups, the Mothers' Union and the Presbyterian Woman's Guild, it was not long before twelve students of KAPE level were enrolled for the two year course. The Mothers' Union and the Presbyterian Woman's Guild asked if they could make the "rules" of the school and very strict they were: No student should leave the YWCA compound without permission and never alone. The Warden should always be told where they were going and how long they would be away. All students should be back in the YWCA by 6 p.m. Should any student break these rules, she would be sent back to her village immediately. Such rules only the mothers in the villages could decree but Edna endeavoured to adhere to them and she made it clear to the girls what would happen if they broke these rules. As demand for accommodation in Beecher House was coming in very slowly, the larger of the two dormitories was reserved for the twelve YWCA students who would be starting their course at the school in the New Year.

The students were to be known as Trainees; their practical training would be given in Beecher House, assisting with catering, cooking, cleaning and laundry under the supervision of Edna Collins. They were expected to pay Shs.150 per year out of which they were given Shs.5 per month pocket money. Had Beecher

Into the New Kenya — 1958

Nativity Play at Ruiru Sisal Estate

House been sharing a kitchen with Windsor House, this project would not have been possible. It was decided that qualified voluntary teachers should be recruited wherever possible to give lessons during the afternoons. The Red Cross agreed to teach Child Care, First Aid, Home Nursing, Nutrition and Hygiene and to enter them for their part 1 and 2 examinations. Singers offered to donate a sewing machine and to send an instructress. At that time the London Council of Domestic Studies examination was taken by Domestic Science students in all Kenya High Schools and the London Council agreed to accept YWCA Trainees. After much correspondence between Edna and London, the Royal Society of Arts agreed to enroll the Trainees for their "English Examination for Foreigners", an examination which hitherto had been taken only by foreigners, in U.K. Further details of this course are set out by Mrs. Gecaga in a letter to Geneva in 1959.

Mr Rodseth of the Ruiru Sisal Estate, son of a Norwegian missionary, was the very caring manager, doing everything possible for the education and development of his African employees. He asked that a YM/YW group be started there and Mary could see that this was a place where joint work was the best possible way of helping these people. On Christmas morning, Mary and Vera drove out to the Sisal Estate to see the YM/YW group performing a Nativity Play.

Residents whose families lived in Kenya went home for Christmas but many remained in the hostels and all joined together for Christmas Dinner at midday in Windsor House dining room.

On 27th December a YM/YW building was opened at Ngewa; this had been organised by the YMCA. The ceremony was attended by the YWCA Colony President, Lady O'Connor, with Mary and Vera. YM/YW groups were now operating in many Kikuyu villages and Vera considered it important that a YWCA presence should be seen, especially as the YMCA had issued badges bearing the name of both Associations. Every Sunday, for the next month 6 months therefore, she set forth with the Rev. James Milroy of the YMCA. and after his departure to Meru, with her driver Thogo, together with any Windsor House residents who were interested, to visit some of these village groups. Sometimes they would spend all day, attending the morning Church Service which would either be Anglican or Presbyterian, being given lunch by the hospitable villagers and meeting nearby groups in the afternoon.

In the village churches in those days, women and children sat on one side and men on the other. Vera would always be welcomed with great courtesy and given a chair by the Altar table. On several occasions, a large basket was passed round for the Collection and as most people in the congregation had more produce than money, sometimes a live chicken would be given as an offering, and at other times eggs, fruit and vegetables. One Sunday, in a Presbyterian Church as the Morning Service was coming to a close, Vera noticed through the unglazed windows an old African man walking with a staff making his way towards the Church. She had also noticed that there was a bowl of water standing on the Communion Table. As the old man entered the Church, a young YMCA member left the front row and went to meet him, and led him to the Minister. Grandfather had come to be baptised and his grandson was his sponsor. To Vera it seemed that she was witnessing a scene from the Acts of the Apostles and she felt privileged to be part of this very moving Service.

On another Sunday, the village schoolmaster and his wife had kindly invited Vera for lunch. As she walked with him from the Church she asked how he liked living in a village, knowing that the villagisation scheme had been enforced during the Emergency. He replied thoughtfully, "We very much enjoy having our village church and the children no longer have to walk many miles to school, but my wife and I are worried because they will play with the children who live in the next house". Vera asked why this was a problem. "They are not Christians" he almost whispered. Feeling that there must be a lesson somewhere, Vera said "Perhaps that is why God allowed you to be put in villages so that Christians could help their neighbours." The good man stood still and after a moment's pause said "Madam, I had never thought of that." Similar comments were made with regard to the YWCA hostels and Vera frequently had to explain that hostels were not for Christian girls only but Christian hostels for all girls.

The YM/YW meetings usually took place in the school after lunch, the local schoolmaster acting as interpreter from Kikuyu to English. Again the men sat on one side and the women and babies on the other. At one of these meetings, Vera asked what happened to all the produce taken in the church collection and she was told that two YWCA members took them to the nearest market on Mondays, bringing the money back for the church funds. Every word had to be translated

Into the New Kenya — 1959

into Kikuyu, so it was difficult to make contact with the women and girls. Vera remembers asking several groups the following questions: Who is your Chairman? Who is your Vice-Chairman? Who is your Secretary? Always these positions were held by men; but the Treasurer was invariably a woman! It was necessary to explain that there was no such World Movement as YM/YW, though both had Headquarters in Geneva. The fact that both were world organisations for young Christians caught the imagination of these young people and many years later, the Provost of All Saints' Cathedral, Nairobi, told Vera that it was through joining his YM/YW village group, that he became a Christian.

Most of the younger women spoke some English and by chatting to them after the meetings it became obvious that they were very interested in the YWCA rather than these mixed groups where they had little or no say; one of these girls, a school teacher, was Jean Ngoima; more about her later.

Vera first encountered the Revival Movement in these villages. The Church services seemed to be very normal and conventional, except for the sermons which lasted a good deal longer than those in European churches. It was at open air meetings and services that she sometimes felt that she was being watched to see if she knew the tunes and English words of the Revival choruses, which indeed, she did not. At first she felt some criticism but soon she became sufficiently familiar with these folk to discuss the Movement and to show an interest. She remembers remarking that the Revival seemed very similar to the revivals instigated by the Old Testament prophets — Isaiah, Jeremiah and others. This made them think and seemed to put things into perspective and soon she knew she had been accepted. It was later that she learnt of the great courage shown during the Emergency by some of these Revival Christians. They, no less than their fellow Africans, wanted independence for their country but were strongly and openly opposed to any sort of violence.

1959. Priority: Education and Training.

In the New Year of 1959, girls began to register for the School. Some came from remote villages and had never seen a two storey building or a staircase. Nor had they seen glass windows, experienced electric light, or modern sanitation. A good deal of careful orientation was necessary before teaching could begin. Soon they were happily settled and comfortably accommodated in the twelve-bedded dormitory. Edna, realising that it would be some time before the hostel was full, offered Vera a bedroom and use of the Reception office, thus bringing a little more revenue to Beecher House. This enabled the National General Secretary to live on the job, set up the first National H.Q. and engage a part-time typist.

Anne Barnett, who had just arrived from London to work with the C.C.K., took over in January from Mrs. Partridge as Warden of Bahati Hostel for one year. She soon became a trusted friend and advisor to the residents.

At a party in the Bishop's garden for the World General Secretary Elizabeth Palmer (fourth from left). With her were (left to right): Mrs Beecher, The Hon Mrs Jemima Gecaga, Mary Suthren, Mrs Jacobs, Lady O'Connor, Mrs Helen Haylett

Minutes of the first Executive Committee meeting of the year state that Mrs Jacobs of the Asian community, had been co-opted and Miss Miriam Janisch had been elected Colony Vice-President. Discussion took place regarding the type of literature which should be accepted and displayed in the hostels. The N.G.S. advised that the YWCA should co-operate fully with the Roman Catholic Church and other Christian denominations and that all literature sent by them should be given full publicity including the Christian Science Monitor. This was agreed. It will be remembered that a similar discussion took place in 1943. Executive considered that the time had come to set up an Education and Training Committee; Elizabeth Normand kindly agreed to take responsibility for this.

At the March meeting, Mary told Executive that she had started a YWCA group at Kitui and she gave good reports about the Y-teens at the African Girls' High School, the Machakos High School and the School for Asian Girls — "The Duchess of Gloucester"; also about the group at Machakos Teacher Training College. Vera reported on a joint CCK/YM/YW Leadership Training Weekend which had been held at the Nairobi Teacher Training College which had been attended by 60 men and 36 women. She also reported that Staff Meetings were now held regularly. The N.G.S. told Executive Committee that she had been one of the speakers at a Convention of Women's Societies, held in Nairobi, the subject being "The African Girl Emerges into Urban Life'. It is interesting to note from Anna Rice's book "A History of World YWCA" that before the turn of the century, a conference had been launched on "The Place of the YWCA in the Social and

Into the New Kenya — 1959

Industrial Awakening". That was Europe in 1899 and it seemed to ring a bell in the Kenya of 1959.

Elizabeth Palmer, World General Secretary, arrived for the official opening of the two new buildings, which took place in Beecher House during the A.G.M. on 10th April 1959 when over 200 people attended. The Bishop of Mombasa opened the proceedings with prayer and the President, Lady O'Connor, who was in the Chair, welcomed Miss Palmer. In her report, the N.G.S. said "Our opportunities are vast, our resources both in manpower and money are limited but I feel confident that if we can work as a team, combining staff, committee members and all well-wishers, we will create a YWCA in this country worthy of the fine heritage of our great World Association".

Trainees working and studying in Beecher House attended the opening ceremony wearing their new YWCA School uniforms. During Miss Palmer's visit, Mrs Beecher very kindly gave a lunch party at Bishopsbourne to which she invited the Executive and chairmen of all Committees.

In May, the Hon. Jemima Gecaga on behalf of the Executive Committee wrote a comprehensive memorandum in which she said "Realising the tremendous need for further education of women in the Colony, Kenya YWCA proposes to make such education its main project during the next four years". She then described the three types of residential courses which were either already operating or in preparation.

1. Courses lasting from four to eight weeks for the wives of educated Africans. These she considered to be of great importance in view of the fact that 'many of these women were left in Kenya whilst their husbands studied abroad and the consequent gap in educational background and culture had been the result'.

Subjects to be covered:

English — oral and written

Dress sense and Dress-making

Hostessing and Catering

Home-making and Budgetting Diet and Nutrition, Child care and Home Nursing.

Civics

Christian Home and Family

The first of these courses was scheduled to take place in October.

2. Courses lasting approximately one week to promote YWCA voluntary leadership within village Associations. "These students would be carefully selected on past merit." Subjects to be covered would include :

How to form a Committee.

How to run a Meeting, Agenda, Minutes etc.

History of YWCA; how to promote a three-fold programme of Body, Mind and Spirit.

Health, Hygiene, Childcare, Diet, and Nutrition.

Budgeting.
Christian Home and Family Life.
Service to the Community.
Agriculture
Co-operation with Governmental Advisory & Welfare bodies.

"These women would normally not be able to afford more than approximately Shs.5 per week, It would therefore be necessary for the YWCA to subsidise."

The first of these courses was scheduled to take place in August.

3. A Vocational Training Scheme lasting two years "…which is already in operation, whereby girls, who had already passed the KAPE but failed to get into High School or Teacher Training College, live in the YWCA. Having had eight years education these girls, left in their villages, become very frustrated. Under supervision these students do the housework, laundry, cooking and sewing in Beecher House thus gaining practical experience. Our aim is to educate these girls so that they feel able to mix with Europeans unselfconsciously and become better wives and mothers and help create a middle-class African home." Every afternoon they have lessons lasting two to three hours covering the following subjects:

Institutional Management.
Cookery, Catering, Menu planning and Nutrition.
English, oral and written.
Needlework, Dressmaking and Handicrafts.
Budgetting and simple Bookkeeping.
Civics and General Knowledge.

The Red Cross had agreed to give classes in Home-Nursing, Child Care, First Aid and Hygiene.

Mrs Gecaga went on to say that these girls had the use of a library and were invited to join in all the educational and social functions within the hostels.

This Memorandum was sent to the World Office in June, supported by the following addendum by the General Secretary of the C.C.K., the Rev. Paul Feuter:

"The three projects mentioned by Mrs. Gecaga are to be highly commended.

Project 1 is very important in view of the number of Africans who go overseas and come back with a tendency to criticise their wives for their lack of education.

Project 2 is springing from the general feeling in our YMCA/YWCA/CCK Committee that training of lay people to take responsible positions in the Church (e. g. Youth Work) is essential.

Project 3 is a completely new scheme and a pioneering work. Much experimenting is still going on. I saw the girls at work last Sunday and they made an excellent impression.

We trust that these and other projects will be a very real contribution to the future of Christian work in this country."

Into the New Kenya — 1959

A YM/YW village group visits All Saint's Cathedral

It was Elizabeth Palmer who suggested that a good way to create interest in the new work which was being set up would be to organise monthly Fork Luncheons to which members of other women's organisations, and ladies from the Consulates and High Commissions could be invited. So began the Beecher House Fork Luncheons, the first being on 1st June. These proved to be very enjoyable, successful and rewarding. Among other organisations, the East African Women's League was invited, and although in those days the League was for Europeans only, many members were eager to become involved with the development of African women. Soon, several of their number became responsible voluntary teachers in the school, and good friends of the Trainees, often inviting them to their homes.

Executive decided that Miss Miriam Janisch, Vice-President, should represent the Association at the YWCA World Council to be held in October, in Mexico. Sincere gratitude was expressed to the YWCA of U.S.A. for generously agreeing to pay her return fare from Kenya. World Office had recommended that during the Council Meeting the Kenya Association should be promoted to Category "C".

Executive Minutes speak of a Sunday afternoon meeting of YM/YW members at Ngewa which was attended by about 400 young men and women. A group of members had volunteered to work in Bahati garden, and the City Parks Department had agreed to advise and help. The Committee was told about a YM/YW Leadership Training Course which had been held at Thogoto Teacher Training College. This was well attended.

During June, Mary Suthren and Edna Collins, with considerable help from committee members, held the first of the residential courses for YWCA village volunteers. Discussion took place regarding Programme material and it was decided that the YWCA should not always rely on YM/YW/CCK but produce some specifically for YWCA members thus giving more emphasis on the development of women's work.

About this time, Windsor/Montgomery House Committee decided that the old single rooms should be upgraded to bring them in line with the new wing. This affected about a dozen residents and necessitated finding accommodation for a period of six to eight weeks. As the top floor of Beecher House was still not full it was decided that it should be rented by the Windsor/Montgomery Committee while these repairs were in progress. It was agreed that these residents would continue to have all their meals in Windsor House. When the time came for them to return to their own rooms they were loath to do so as they had enjoyed the experience of living in a multi-racial community and had made new friends.

In July, the N.G.S. told the Executive that Isabel Apindi would be representing Kenya at the British Council of Churches Conference to be held in Oxford from 7th to 26th September, the subject being "Social Development in the family." The invitation from the B.C.C. to send a woman delegate, had been sent to the C.C.K. Fortunately, Vera had been present at the meeting when it was stated that there was no African woman as yet sufficiently experienced to attend. Vera told the meeting that there were several YWCA members who would make excellent delegates. She was then told that a reply had to be in the post within three days. Assuring the Committee that they would have the name of a suitable woman before then, she discussed the matter with Mary and Edna and they decided to telephone Isabel Apindi the next morning. Isabel, of course, was more than willing to accept, pending permission from the Probation Service; this was obtained the same day. Phoebe Asiyo was in U.K., having been a delegate at the Conference in Edinburgh of "Country Women of the World" and Mrs Ang'awa from Mombasa, was about to go to England to take a course. The NGS therefore

Into the New Kenya — 1959

sent the names of these three members to Janet Little, Head of the International Department of Great Britain, asking her to make contact.

At the next meeting of Executive, Vera reported that she had approached the Assistant Chief Secretary asking that Isabel be granted two extra weeks following the Oxford Conference to give her the opportunity to see something of Probation work in England. This had been granted and Executive Committee agreed to give Isabel £5 to enable her to stay one week at the YWCA Headquarters Hostel, in Baker Street, London. Later in the year, the General Secretary of the C.C.K. told Vera that the B.C.C. had considered that Miss Apindi had made a very useful contribution to the Oxford Conference.

Sir Patrick Renison had arrived as the new Governor and during an interview, Lady Renison had told the Press that one of her main interests was the YWCA as she had been closely involved with the Association in both British Honduras and British Guiana.

The Executive Committee asked the N. G. S to make an appointment to visit Government House as soon as possible. Lady Renison was extremely interested to hear about the work being done in Kenya and agreed to become Patron, saying she would like to be "an active one."

A circular letter arrived from the C.C.K. in February stating that there was a scheme called Voluntary Service Overseas whereby boys aged about 18, straight from school, would be sent to developing countries to assist as volunteers in educational and welfare work for one year under the auspices of Inter-Church Aid. The N.G.S. telephoned the General Secretary of the C.C.K. the Rev. Paul Feuter, saying that the YWCA would welcome a female volunteer. The reply was that no girls had been offered. Vera suggested that a letter be sent immediately to Janet Lacey, Director of Inter-Church Aid. The outcome of this was that Bronwyn Quint, one of the first two female V.S.O.s to be recruited and the first to be sent to Africa, arrived on September 16th. She was a great success, working in the school and helping Mary with her group work. She was a favourite with the Trainees, being much the same age, and, on her one free weekend each month, she would invariably be invited to go home to a village with one of them and stay with their families.

The first visitor from another African Association was Mrs. Agnes Dhulula from Bulawayo. She was given a warm welcome and shown some of the work which was taking place in Nairobi.

In October, the YWCA was given permission to hold a Flag Day in Nairobi. This raised £304 and was distributed as follows:

£50 to each of the three hostels, £70 towards World Council expenses and £84 towards a tearoom which the Anglican Church had asked the Association to open in Church House. This was to be rent free until March 1960 by which time it would

Bronwyn Quint, the first female VSO to be sent to East Africa, giving and English lesson to trainees in Beecher House dining room

be determined if such a facility was needed. On 1st December Mary and Edna organised the opening and Mrs. Everitt was appointed manageress.

It was becoming evident that money with which to build a National Headquarters with a Conference Room, offices and staff flats, must somehow be found. The N.G.S., discussed this with the President and Bishop Beecher, and it was decided to launch an Appeal. A good friend of the Bishop's, whose wife happened to be on the Windsor/Montgomery House Committee, was asked to become Chairman. This was the well known E. T. Jones, affectionately known as "Jonah". He had recently retired as head of Shell, East Africa. This Committee was to be known as Appeals and Publicity and aimed to raise £2,000 a year over the next three years.

On the 28th October the Mayor of Nairobi Mrs. Needham-Clark, launched the Appeal by giving a Reception in her Parlour. The Rev. Dishon Mwangoli was the Mayor's Chaplain, this being the first time that an African priest had held the appointment. The YWCA's platform for requesting funds was to raise the status of women, the U. N. O. having just reported on their Commission on that subject. Furthermore the W.C.C. were about to set up a Department for "Men and Women working together"; there was at that time a conference in London organised by the Colonial Office on "Social Development through the Family" and the C.C.K. had decided to make their 1960 project "The Christian Home and Family".

Into the New Kenya — 1959

Another important factor was that building costs were still low, and it was rumoured that very soon these costs would be rising. Money came in steadily but too slowly, so Vera suggested to the Bishop that she should write to Janet Lacey, Director of Inter-Church Aid, and ask for a loan of £5,000 interest free, for 3 years, by which time it was almost certain that the money could be repaid from the Appeal Fund. Fortunately the loan was granted and negotiated through C.C.K.

The N.G.S. was asked to draw a rough plan for the National Building and submit it to the architect. Vera remembered that when discussing the possibility of a National H.Q. with Elizabeth Palmer, she had been advised to build on as large a scale as possible, as the need for office space was bound to expand. Two staff flats were urgently required at that time, but might not be in the future. The final plan was for a Conference Room with toilet and a small kitchen on the ground floor, together with a storeroom and three offices. Above, were two offices and two flats, all of which had connecting doors, thus enabling flats or parts of flats to become offices if and when required. The architect was asked to prepare working drawings and work commenced on the foundations. It was most fortunate that Janet Lacey happened to be on one of her visits to Kenya and she laid the foundation stone which reads:

"This stone was laid on December 12th, 1959

by Janet Lacey

Director of Inter-Church Aid and Refugee Services for the British Council of Churches"

Mary now had eleven YWCA groups in Kikuyu villages, seven of which she and a volunteer, Mrs. Evie McIver, visited regularly, and the other four were run by African women volunteers trained by Mary. Groups were also going well in the African Girls' High School, the Asian Girls' High School and the Delamere Girls' High School, which was a European Day School. This was good news for it was evidence that YWCA was being offered to girls of all races in Kenya. Mary estimated that there were approximately 100 paid-up YWCA members in the country, an increase of 70 since 1955.

More good news of a different sort was to come; Nairobi City Council had generously given a donation of £125 to Bahati and £200 to Beecher House, and a grant of £2000 had been received from World YWCA for training purposes.

The YM/YW Week of Prayer and World Fellowship had been very successful. Members of the YMCA and YWCA took turns in giving the morning religious broadcast "Thought for the Day" on K.B.C. and, on the final Sunday afternoon, a Service was held in All Saints Cathedral. Twenty five buses and lorries brought about 1,000 YM/YW members in from the villages. African, European and Asian Clergy officiated and the Bishop preached. The service sheets were printed in English and Kikuyu.

Rickshaws to Jets

In November, Gwyneth Jackson went on her first long leave of three months, leaving the very efficient Deputy Warden, Eve Middleton in charge.

When Windsor House Committee started to discuss their 1959 annual Christmas Market, the N.G.S. suggested that Beecher House Committee should join them in this event. Vera felt that it was high time that these two committees started to do some work together, as she had in mind the time, in the not too distant future, when there would be only one Hostel Committee. The Market was organised by the two committees and held in the Motor Mart on a Saturday morning. £300 was raised — £220 more than in 1958.

The School was going well with a volunteer teaching staff of over twenty, many of whom were members of the E.A.W.L. Applications were coming in from all over East Africa. Twelve girls were selected, to start as "Junior" Trainees in January 1960. These were all from Kenya but from various tribes. This meant finding accommodation for them. Beecher House was still not full, the less expensive beds being in most demand. It was decided, therefore, that in the New Year the School should occupy both dormitories and that some of the single rooms should be converted into doubles thus reducing the rates. This met the requirements of both Hostel and School at that time. A subsidy was paid by Beecher House towards running the School because the Trainees did all the domestic work making it unnecessary to employ staff. It was estimated that the saving on wages would cover the expenses of twelve more students.

A training weekend organised jointly by YM/YW at the request of the Community Development Officer, Nyeri, was held for Government Youth Leaders. 30 young men and women attended, a third of whom were Roman Catholic. On the first evening, an American Roman Catholic Father had been present, together with clergy from other Christian denominations. This was the first real contact the YM/YW had had with the R. C. Church in Kenya and it was surprising how little the Catholic delegates knew about the Protestants and vice versa. At first the students sat in their "Church" groups. One young man, a Roman Catholic, asked the Father "Would it be all right for me to say the 'Our Father' with my brother over there?" To which the Priest replied "Nothing but good ever came out of saying the 'Our Father' together." It was indeed an informative and memorable weekend.

The Mombasa Association reported good progress. Helen Haylett had been elected President on the retirement of Barbara Greenwood. An inter-racial group met regularly and educational work with African women and girls was expanding very successfully under the guidance of Kitty Hall. Committee members gave cooking classes in their own kitchens as the Hostel kitchen was too busy. The Committee was searching for a suitable property to rent or buy for a lower income hostel for African girls working at the Coast; this was at the request of the C.C.K. The Mombasa Committee was under the impression that their hostel was situated on a site reserved for Europeans only. Vera therefore asked Helen to go to the Bank and study the Deeds. On examining them, Helen was so delighted that she telephoned Vera with the good news that nothing concerning race was mentioned. As in Nairobi, only European girls were earning enough to live in the high income hostel, which was of a very high standard and making money for the Association, the fees being Shs.440 per month.

When the Mombasa Committee became aware that the police were now permitted to have their wives living with them in the Police Compound, they realised what tremendous problems these women were having in communicating with one another, coming as they did, from many different tribes and usually speaking only their tribal language. Kitty Hall therefore obtained permission to set up educational and recreational programmes in the Compound, priority being given to classes in Swahili.

Meru was also doing well. Keith Foot, the District Officer, had been working with Alice Nkilote and a good YM/YW group had been established. Together with the YMCA N.G.S. Vera went to Meru for an enrolment service of 30 young men and women. This time Mount Kenya was visible in all its magnificence, the white glaciers glistening in the sunshine against the blue sky.

Christmas 1959 was indeed a memorable one because it was agreed that any resident from any of the three Nairobi Hostels in the YWCA on Christmas Day, would be invited to midday Christmas Dinner in Windsor House. Although many girls went home or to friends, a good proportion remained and what made history was that Anne Barnett brought about six residents from Bahati. After a very jolly meal, everyone moved into Windsor House Lounge until tea time and Christmas Cake. The first multi-racial Christmas. A really happy day.

1960. National Headquarters Building opens

1960 was a very important year for the Association, for Margaret Kariuki joined the staff, being the first African to hold a senior post in the Kenya YWCA. Margaret was the younger daughter of the first Kikuyu Anglican Bishop and she had agreed to work for the YWCA when she returned from her studies in England. Her post was Deputy Warden Beecher House and Assistant Headmistress of the School. She worked happily with Edna and became a very valuable member of staff. Her salary was paid from a World YWCA grant which was specifically for African staff. She was installed in time to welcome twelve new Trainees — the Juniors.

Anne Barnett, having completed her year, resigned as Warden Bahati to take up full time work with the C.C.K. Anne, who had been doing part time with the C.C.K. had become acquainted with an African couple, Mr and Mrs Leonard Kabunja, who she felt would make splendid Wardens. As they were not immediately available, Mrs Garriock became Warden and was joined a few months later by Mr and Mrs Kabunja.

World H.Q. asked the N.G.S. to visit Dar-es-Salaam in January to determine whether or not a YWCA was required in Tanganyika, as it was then called. Sir Richard Turnbull was the Governor at that time and his wife was keen for the Association to open a hostel in Dar-es-Salaam. Sir Richard was able to arrange an appointment for Vera to meet Mr. Julius Nyerere who was shortly to become the first President. Having travelled widely, he knew about the YWCA and was all in favour of an Association setting up in his country and assured Vera that it would have his blessing. Dag Hammarskjoeld, Secretary General to the United Nations happened to be giving a lecture in Dar-es-Salaam at that time and Vera was very fortunate in being invited to attend. Vera's Report to Geneva resulted in Clary Elfing a member of the Swedish YWCA staff, arriving in Dar-es Salaam the following October.

Early in 1960, the Bishop, together with the Colony President, called an important extraordinary meeting of the Executive and Windsor/Montgomery House Committees and the Trustees. Bishop Beecher told the meeting that the Appeal was going well but that he and the President did not consider that the YWCA should be appealing to the general public for funds unless all its operations were contributing to the work of the Association. It was therefore recommended that the financial policy should be revised. The only profit making concern was Windsor/Montgomery House and it was decided that these profits should be channelled into the expansion of work throughout the country. The Mombasa Hostel would also be asked to contribute. When it became known that all the profits of the high income hostel were to be used for developing work with African women and girls, a Hostel Committee member told the N.G.S. that she considered this to be unfair. Vera explained that it should be regarded as being similar to income tax, better off people subsidising the less well off. She went on to explain that in the YWCA it was essential that all work together for the good of the Association as a whole and that any hostel opposing this practice should not display the Blue Triangle. Vera hoped that she had not caused offence. She need not have worried; the conversation had apparently caused an awakening for, many years after Independence, this good member continued to serve loyally.

On her return from Tanganyika, the N.G.S. was instructed to draw up a new Constitution with the guidance of a solicitor, incorporating the new policy, to be ready for the first National Council which would be meeting in July. The NGS deliberately wrote into the Constitution that there should be two National meetings a year, a one-day Council and a residential Convention to last two or three days. Some members of the Executive considered this to be extravagant but Vera explained that both would be training experiences with the aim of building a Nationwide Movement as quickly as possible. Branches would be asked to elect their Councillors from members who had attended the previous Convention, thus ensuring that they understood their responsibilities.

Into the New Kenya — 1960

Vera was informed by Geneva that a YWCA group had already been started in Ashira T.T.C. at Marangu in the Moshi District of Tanganyika by Elizabeth Mswia, a young school teacher who had become a member of the Association while studying in America. World YWCA had heard of this from missionaries passing through Geneva and Vera was asked to contact Elizabeth. After consulting Executive Committee, it was decided that Elizabeth should be invited to attend a YM/YW training course which would be taking place in Nairobi during the Easter school holidays and asked to stay on for the YWCA World Membership Day celebrations when twelve Africans and fifteen Europeans were to be enrolled as Full Members. Elizabeth would be the guest of the Kenya Association. She was delighted to accept and her visit enabled her to make arrangements for Vera's visit to Marangu later in the year.

In Nairobi, the International Club, whose members included Africans, Asians, Americans, and Europeans from Britain and Germany, were still meeting regularly and the Junior Group continued to be very popular; both met in the Whitehouse Road Hut. Groups in the High Schools and Teacher Training Colleges continued to flourish. The African Girls' High School group now had seventy enrolled members. They had a splendid chairman, Rosemary Kairu, who even then knew she wanted a career in Social Work; more about her later.

In February Mary went on a working safari to Nyanza, speaking to several groups in Teacher Training Colleges and Schools and visiting the flourishing Kisumu Branch.

Gwyneth Jackson returned from long leave, having spent several days with World YWCA in Geneva. She found the Hostel full and running smoothly under the Chairmanship of Mrs. Eve Ross and in the capable hands of the Assistant Warden Mrs. Middleton and Housekeeper Mrs. Venn, "Mid" and "Ven".

Mrs. Betty Montgomery, now Mrs. Stratton, asked that the new wing of the original Hostel should no longer bear her former name and she suggested that the whole building be called International House. After some discussion with the Windsor/Montgomery House Committee this suggestion was taken to Executive and accepted. This meant that any girl who could afford the fees was welcome to live there. It is interesting to note that there is no Minute declaring the Hostel to be multi-racial and indeed it was some years before African girls' salaries were sufficiently high to pay the rates required. The new name was very apt however, because tourists from many parts of the world were arriving and taking any bed that might be available.

International House Committee considered that the kitchen premises and bathrooms needed to be modernised and more bathrooms built. The bathrooms were to be situated at the south end of the hostel and would provide facilities for 30 residents. These were to serve an important purpose in future years. As International House was full, an extension was required to the dining-room. The estimated cost for this work was £7,000. An extension to the Reception was also recommended, including new cloakrooms; this would cost a further £1,200. Fortunately the Hostel Committee had sufficient in their reserves to pay for all this.

There is a letter in World YWCA files from Gwyneth Jackson telling Janet Thomson that prayers were held in the Hostel every Sunday morning which the servants attended. Most people went to Church, the Anglican Trainees going to All Saints Cathedral, the Presbyterians and Methodists to St. Andrew's, and girls belonging to other denominations, usually attended Nairobi Chapel. Prayers were held in the School every week-day at 10.15 taken either by Edna Collins or Margaret Kariuki to which everyone was welcome. Trainees were also given weekly Bible Study.

The School now had twelve Seniors and twelve Juniors; every Senior was linked with a Junior with whom to work and this proved to be very beneficial. A rota of Prefects was organised, whereby two Seniors took office for a period of one month twice in their second year. Prefects were given special responsibilities, authority and privileges thus helping the girls to gain confidence. During the Trainees' second term as prefects, the N.G.S. always invited them for dinner in her flat. By then the girls were completely relaxed and bursting with questions; invariably the encyclopaedia had to be brought out. It was always a very happy occasion. Once Vera was asked if there were any farms in England; she replied that of course there were. "Who works on them, Africans?" The colonial way of life had certainly instilled some very false concepts; these girls couldn't imagine a European getting his hands dirty or his boots muddy. Some years later, two girls stayed on a working farm in Somerset, England, as guests of friends of Vera's; there they encountered plenty of hard work and mud.

The 24 Trainees were sleeping in the two dormitories and Beecher House was full, with a waiting list. This meant that the N.G.S. had to find alternative accommodation for herself and her office. Early in March, she decided to occupy the smaller of the two, now empty, wooden huts, known as the "Prefabs". Here she had two bedrooms, a sitting-room, a bathroom and two offices. Having no telephone made life very difficult; Vera was constantly running over to Reception at one or other of the hostels to receive calls. National Headquarters had to remain in this hut until the HQ building was ready for occupation. There is a letter in Geneva files to Elizabeth Palmer from Vice-President Miriam Janisch saying that the provision of a part-time secretary for Miss Harley has helped to reduce the mountains of paper through which she has literally to wade in the Army Hut Office, while the National Office is being built. "I greatly hope that under the generous grant for training it will soon be possible for a full-time secretary to be appointed".

There was now a joint YM/YW/CCK Committee and in May, news came that Inter-Church Aid had granted the Committee £3500 a year for the next 4 years, with which to organise a leadership training team. Both World Offices and British Associations

Into the New Kenya — 1960

The National HQ and staff flats opened in June 1960

were seeking for the right staff to head up this important project, which was to be colony wide, serving any Church or Youth Group needing assistance.

Mary ran a 10 day Leadership Training course in Mombasa in May.

She returned to find the National Block ready for occupation and it was time to choose colour schemes. In a letter to her sister Vera wrote "Very attractive curtain material was bought costing between Shs.5 and Shs.10 per yard". The Trainees, assisted by Edna and Mary, made and hung the curtains and various committee members searched Nairobi salerooms for inexpensive furniture for the the two staff flats. It was not until Mary and Vera had moved in that they realised what a magnificent view there was every evening from their balcony. Near sunset, Nairobi offered a silhouette of rare beauty, all the buildings appearing to have turned to gold in the clear equatorial light.

In June Vera reminded the Executive that $2,000 had been received from World YWCA for training purposes. She suggested that the two pre-fabs should be retained to accommodate students taking short residential courses. This was agreed.

On 30th June, Lady Renison, the Patron, performed the opening ceremony of the National Head Quarters Building before a company of over a hundred guests. Graham Hyslop, the man who was later to compose the Kenya National Anthem (the inspiration said to have come from a Giriama folk song), brought his portable organ and everyone sang lustily. Mary and Vera moved into their respective flats and as only three offices were required at that time, the room on the left of the steps and the storeroom behind were used by the Girl Guides who had lent £500, interest free, on that condition. Betty Tweedie, an International House resident and a Full Member, who for many years had been a loyal volunteer to Mary with her African group work, moved in with Mary, renting as her bedroom the room behind the N.G.S. 's office at the top of the steps and sharing Mary's flat.

At the beginning of July, a letter arrived from the N.G.S. of the YWCA. of the Federal Republic of Germany saying that their members were very interested in the Kenya Association and were launching a "Kenya" Appeal, and she hoped to be able to send £1,000 a year for the next three years. She said that the enthusiasm of their members was quite remarkable. Executive were extremely grateful for this meant that the expenses for the NGS's second term would be covered.

Lady O'Connor said that she would be in England for several months and, as her husband would be retiring in 1961, they would be leaving Kenya. She therefore asked that her resignation should be tendered to Council in July. A Vice-President, Mrs Ruth Newbold, was asked to stand in for Lady O'Connor until elections at Council.

The first meeting of the constitutionally elected National Council which was to replace the A.G.M. was held in the new Conference Room on 5th July 1960 and was chaired by Vice-President Miriam Janisch, Vice-President Mrs Newbold being unwell. The Bishop of Mombasa, opened the meeting with prayer. Delegates attended from Nairobi, Mombasa, Kisumu, Meru, Kakamega and from the YM/YW Groups in the Kiambu District. Also from the African Girls' High School, Machakos High School and Teacher Training College. Apologies were received from Lady O'Connor and from Mrs. Helen Haylett, Chairman of Mombasa. Reporting on the resignation of Lady O'Connor, the Bishop said that he knew that he would be expressing the wish of Council in paying tribute to her since as the first Colony President, she had served with such warmth and sensitivity. Council asked that their thanks and best wishes be extended to Lady O'Connor.

The new Constitution, which the N.G.S. had drafted under the guidance of Michael Harley of Hamilton, Harrison and Matthews, the Association's Hon. Legal Advisors, was discussed and adopted. This gave Council authority to set up any Standing Committee which the Executive Committee considered to be necessary for carrying out the programme for the ensuing year.

The Bishop recommended that the Finance Committee, of which he was Chairman, should be dissolved and that Executive should be given the responsibility for Finance and General Purposes. The Board of Trustees would continue to take responsibility for all properties, loans and investment. The Colony President would be ex-officio on the Board.

The following Standing Committees were established: Hostels, Education and Training, Programme and Membership, Appeals and Publicity and African Estates.

Into the New Kenya — 1960

Lady Harragin was elected Colony President. Mrs Hannah Rubia, Mrs Phoebe Asiyo, Mrs Kanta Patel and Mrs. Ernestine Kiano were elected to Executive.

The N.G.S., in her Report to Council, recounted how eighteen months ago Bishop Beecher, when thanking Elizabeth Palmer for visiting Kenya, had said that she had "stretched our imagination beyond our Hostel and Group Work enabling us to see that our duty was to create a National Movement worthy of membership within the World Wide Christian Family of the YWCA. "This", she said, "is a very special Council because for the first time the meeting is taking place in our own National Head Quarters. The completion of this building is a coming together of all our efforts, a symbol of our faith in the Kenya YWCA of the future". She told Council that the building, furnishings and car park had cost approximately £6,000. The YWCA of Altrincham, England, had very kindly sent a donation which had been put towards equipment for the Conference Room kitchen. She continued by saying that the Appeal was going well and that it was generally agreed that the School was a great success. Three students had passed the British Red Cross First Aid, Home Nursing and Child Care examinations being the only African candidates. Speaking of the hostels she reminded Council that International House had a large outstanding debt to Nairobi City Council. Fortunately the Hostel was fully occupied, Beecher House was 80 per cent full and Bahati was full with a waiting list. The N.G.S. thanked Anne Barnett for the valuable contribution she had made to Bahati and welcomed Mrs Garriok and Mr and Mrs Kabunja to the staff. The work in the villages and townships was going well as were the High School and College Groups.

Mrs Michael Wood had become Chairman of the Tea Room Committee and was giving great support to Mrs Everett, the hard working Manageress. Mrs Holden had very kindly arranged with Unga Flour Co. for African girls to be trained to make cakes on Unga premises. A profit of £50 had been made during the first ten months.

The Mombasa Association was progressing very satisfactorily, educational classes were being held in the Hostel and in Committee members homes. The various groups in the area were well attended. In response to the request made by the C. C. K in 1959 to open a small hostel at the Coast for African Girls, a flat had been rented for three months, but as there had been no applicants, the experiment had been discontinued. The Mombasa Committee, however, considered that the experience had been of value.

Miss Harley thanked the Trustees, all committee members, friends and Staff for their help and co-operation. In paying special tribute to the retiring Colony President, the N.G.S. said that Lady O'Connor had made her feel very welcome on her arrival in Kenya in 1958 and had given her wonderful guidance, support and friendship ever since and she ended by saying that over the past 105 years the YWCA had been given tremendous opportunities throughout the world, but she doubted if there had ever been a greater opportunity than in Kenya in 1960. The Report was received with great interest and the Bishop voiced on behalf of the National Council, the thankfulness of the Association for the growth of the work under the guidance of Miss Harley and her supporting staff. He then closed the meeting with prayer.

The N.G.S., together with the YMCA N.G.S., was invited by Mr. Tom Mboya to the opening of the new Trades Union Building. They were encouraged to know that the Associations were beginning to be recognised by the people of the "New" Kenya.

On 30th July Thogo drove Alice Nklote of Meru, Doreen Boedeker and the N.G.S. left to Marangu in northern Tanganyika where Elizabeth Mswia had arranged accommodation. They had an excellent meeting on the Saturday morning with the 40 young women at the T.T.C. which constituted the YWCA Group. It was apparent to Doreen, Alice and Vera that these girls had a good knowledge of the Movement with a well balanced programme. In the afternoon, the Group organised a splendid tea party in the College garden. Elizabeth explained that there was also a Group of rural women who she had prepared and who wished to be enrolled as Full Members; they lived on the coffee estates south of Mount Kilamanjaro and met regularly. Elizabeth had arranged for the Enrolment Service to take place in the old Lutheran Church situated on the Southern slopes of the Mountain after the Sunday morning service. Because the rural women spoke only their tribal language, the service sheet had been prepared in Chagga as well as in English. Vera recalled waiting with the African Priest in the large open porch outside the west door of the Church, admiring the magnificent view over the coffee plantation to the distant highlands of southern Tanganyika, watching the would-be YWCA members, often with a baby on their back, slowly wending their way, from many directions, along the paths between the coffee, colourful figures against the dark green bushes, up the hill to the Church, while the local brass band played inside. It was a wonderful Service and a very memorable occasion.

On 3rd August the Church of the Province of East Africa was inaugurated and Bishop Beecher became the first Archbishop of the Province.

In August Bronwyn Quint, the V.S.O. together with Prisca Natui, who was Chairman of the YWCA at Machakos Teacher Training College, attended a World Council of Churches International Work Camp at Bulawayo. They were funded by World YWCA. On 10th September, a farewell tea party was held for Bronwyn; everyone was sad to see her go. She had set a very high standard for V.S.O. and had done splendid work, especially with the Trainees.

A few days later, Elizabeth Forbes and Jean Hollingsworth arrived and were given a great welcome. They soon fitted in and did some excellent work. Elizabeth, being a Girl Guide, started a YWCA Company. She also took the Trainees for swimming lessons once a week at the YMCA Swimming Pool by

Into the New Kenya — 1960

VSOs Elizabeth Forbes and Jean Hollingsworth teach trainees swimming

courtesy of the YMCA. Elizabeth encouraged the girls to play netball, having posts erected on the tennis courts.

At the September Executive a letter was read from the YWCA in Kampala stating that two of their members had not been permitted to stay in the Nairobi Hostel. The N.G.S. said that she had replied that this could not have been the case and she asked the Uganda YWCA to advertise the fact that girls of all races were welcome in Beecher and International House in Nairobi and also in the Mombasa Hostel.

On 27th October, the first course for the wives of educated Africans was organised by the Education and Training Committee; these became known as the Good Hostess Courses. This course lasted for six weeks, and was for politicians' wives. The twelve students were accommodated in the larger wooden "prefab". Breakfast and dinner were taken in Beecher House where they experienced self service, and lunch was taken in Windsor House with waiter service. The syllabus covered the variety of subjects listed in Mrs. Gecaga's memorandum. Visits to the Family Planning clinic in Nairobi were arranged for those students who desired this service. On the last Friday of the Course, the students organised a tea party, inviting their husbands, sending out invitations, cooking cakes, making sandwiches and each wearing the dress which she had made during the course.

Mrs Damaris Ayodo, who had represented Kenya YWCA in 1955 in Kampala, was a student on this first Good Hostess Course and in the following November Mary was delighted to be invited to stay with her in Kisii to meet the YWCA group which she had started.

On 4th October 1960 Clary Elfing arrived from Swedish YWCA and stayed with the Association in Nairobi for three days en route for Dar-es-Salaam where she was to take up her post as first National General Secretary, YWCA Tanganyika.

All Nairobi hostels were full with waiting lists, and Beecher House was asking for the use of the 2 dormitories occupied by 24 Trainees. Meanwhile Edna and Margaret continued to run the school with great efficiency, Beecher House dining room and lounge being used as classrooms every afternoon. Edna told Vera that she felt that the Trainees would benefit if they had properly equipped classrooms; she also considered that they should have a Common Room of their own. Miss McHugh, director of Domestic Science for the Ministry of Education had congratulated the YWCA on the high standard of the school. The N.G.S. decided that she should discuss this with the National President and the Chairman of the Trustees. The consequence was that an extraordinary meeting of Trustees and Executive was called on 17 October, chaired by the Archbishop. He explained that the V.T.S. was now well established and running satisfactorily but that it lacked proper accommodation and facilities. He and the President recommended that a residential Homecraft Training School should be built for 24 students at the estimated cost of £7,500 plus furnishings

There was still a small amount in the Building Fund but the main money would have to be raised. Vera knew that World YWCA might be able to interest another National Association in an educational project, so she wrote to Janet Thomson for advice.

In November and December, the senior Trainees of the V.T.S. were taking their final examinations. Already applications for places for the next intake in January were coming in from all over East Africa. As English was the language in which the Trainees were being taught, they were encouraged to speak in English and not their tribal language. The Education and Training Committee chaired by Elizabeth Normand, decided that as many different tribes as possible should be included in the 1961 intake, but again from Kenya only.

Both the YMCA and the YWCA had been asked to open a multi-racial hostel in Nakuru. After several visits, the two National General Secretaries concluded that the need was acute but small. In November therefore, a house was rented and accommodation provided for twenty men and women. This was very successfully staffed by a married couple from Sweden. Mr and Mrs Garvars. The Guest House opened with six men but only one girl; two more girls were due at the end of the year.

On St. Andrew's Day, the Archbishop's wife, Gladys Beecher, who was a Vice-President, invited all Committee members, Volunteers and staff to a Retreat at Bishopsbourne. It was to be from 11.30 a.m. until 4 p.m. so that people could come and go as convenient. The day began with a short Service in the Archbishop's chapel followed by a relaxing time in the garden, then lunch. It was

Into the New Kenya — 1960

the same pattern during the afternoon with tea at 3.30. Everyone felt that it had been a very beneficial day and sincere gratitude was expressed to Mrs. Beecher.

At the December Executive meeting, it was agreed that the N.G.S. should have a full-time secretary. The Committee and the Trustees decided that a fully equipped Domestic Science School should be built and Edna and her Committee assisted the architect in drawing plans. It was to comprise a laundry, sewing room equipped with a sewing machine which Singers had kindly promised to donate, domestic science room with facilities for cooking by kerosene and electricity. The E.A.P.&L offered to send their senior demonstrator, Miss Giles to give a two-hour lesson each week in cooking by electricity. The Trainees already had experience of cooking by Afro Gas in the Beecher House kitchen. There was also to be a Trainees' Common room and Principal's office all on the ground floor. Above, were dormitories to sleep 24, a staff flat for the Principal, a bed-sitting-room for her Assistant, and twenty single rooms for letting on the second floor. As building costs were still low, and as there was some money in the Building Fund, it was decided that work should begin immediately. The cost would be reduced because no bathrooms were necessary, the single rooms being on the same level as the new bathrooms in International House, to which an entrance would be made. The 24 Trainees would also use these bathrooms, they however, would have to go up a flight of stairs. This new staircase was to be of concrete with iron railings and would be continued to the ground floor, thus acting as a much needed fire escape. The door at the bottom, if locked, would have, on the wall inside, a key in a glass case. This precaution was essential as the only staircase was the original wooden one in Windsor House, and the rope ladders from the wooden verandah in the old hostel were no longer in existence. The new building came to be known as "Bridge Block"; being the bridge connecting the two hostels.

Now it was time to find jobs for the first graduates from the V.T.S. who were due to leave in January. The N.G.S. telephoned the Ministry of Labour and told them that there were twelve girls looking for jobs quoting the list of accredited examinations which they had taken. The European to whom she spoke said "What, African Girls?" Vera said "Yes and we are hoping that you will find work for them." The Director of Langata Women's Prison, who was an American, telephoned to say that she could employ them all as teachers to the non-dangerous inmates. The girls were delighted as having lived together in the YWCA for two years, they were loath to be separated. They were all taken by the driver, Thogo, to the prison for interviews and to see what accommodation they would be given. They returned very disgruntled and Edna was rather worried at their silence. Driver Thogo, a father figure to the Trainees, went to the N. G. S., obviously perplexed. He said they sang on the way there and cried on the way back! As they were still silent the next morning, the N.G.S. asked Violet Wanjiri, a natural leader, to come to her office and explained that the girls need not work in the prison if they didn't want to, but she must be told what had happened. After some pause Violet, said that they had no intention of accepting the posts as they did not like their lavatories. Vera asked what was wrong with them. "There are no pull & let goes," replied Violet. There were in fact no flush toilets in the prison at that time. Vera had to telephone the Director and tell her why none of the girls wished to work at the prison. She was exasperated and asked Vera if she had ever been to an African village; the reply was "many times". "Well then" said the Director "you know that they have no sanitation". Vera then tried to explain that for two years these students had become used to modern sanitation. Edna and Vera were secretly proud of the girls for refusing to drop standards. This was the sort of attitude that was very important for women to adopt in the new Kenya. A year later Vera was told that modern sanitation had been installed in the Women's Prison. Perhaps it was the YWCA Trainees who made the authorities see the need. Four years later, Tabitha Adjiambo, a graduate from the school accepted a post on the staff of Langata Prison working under an African Director.

The Trainees began to realise that they would have to separate to find work. Two places were found as Assistant Hostel Wardens in the YWCA hostels, three as Club Leaders in the villages. Mr. Michael Wood, the Surgeon/Director of AMREF, the Flying Doctor Service, asked if two could go on a land safari with his team to Tanganyika to give lessons in Child Care etc. to village women wherever the team stopped to carry out their work. These two girls, Lilian Njeri and Leah Wangeri, received an excellent report from AMREF and on returning took over Mary's village work. Alison Shrubsole, Principal of Machakos Teacher Training College, was the first Government employee to recognise that the YWCA school was of a high standard and when her European housekeeper/matron retired for health reasons, she appointed two YWCA graduates, one as housekeeper/caterer and the other as matron; they were thus launched as independent professionals.

All the students were now placed, some doing non-residential jobs in Nairobi in which case they continued to live in Beecher House as residents.

The joint YM/YW work was going well. The Rev. James Milroy was working in Meru where Alice Nkilote was being of great assistance.

There were now 40 YM/YW Groups in the Kiambu District of which 34 met regularly every week. James Gathuri was being paid by the YMCA to co-ordinate this work. On the Sunday of the YM/YW Week of Prayer and World Fellowship there was again a Mass Rally at All Saints Cathedral, buses and trucks bringing Members from the Kiambu District. Service sheets were printed in Kikuyu and English. The Archbishop preached and clergy of all denominations participated.

The Technical College had become The Royal College and a YWCA Vice-President Miss Miriam Janisch was appointed Warden of the Women's Halls of Residence. She invited the NGS to speak to the students about the YWCA and

Into the New Kenya — 1960

before long a good group was formed. Once a month, Vera used to go for dinner at the College and a YWCA Meeting would be held afterwards. The chairman was Susan Thumbe; more about her later.

The Girls' Friendly Society wrote to Mrs. Beecher from London saying that they proposed starting a branch in Kenya; being an Anglican society, they sought her support. She brought the matter to YWCA Executive and it was decided that they should be advised to open in the Taita District where there was little chance of starting YWCA work. To this they agreed and a G. F. S. worker arrived from England and was warmly welcomed in the Hostel. Co-Membership GFS/YW was established.

On 2nd December a very successful Christmas Fair was held on the beautiful terrace of the City Hall. This event was chaired by Mrs Don Small, a member of the Appeals and Publicity Committee, and raised over £1,000.

Christmas celebrations were as in 1959. Residents and their friends from all three Nairobi hostels were welcomed for midday dinner in the attractive Windsor House Dining room followed by tea in the big lounge.

During 1960 the Emergency Regulations were finally lifted having been in force for eight years.

1961. Bridge Block and School Building open.
Ofafa Hotel becomes a YWCA Centre.

World YWCA organised the first All African YWCA conference in Salisbury University (now Harare) from 28th December 1960 to 10th January 1961. Kenya was invited to send six delegates and the following were elected: Maggie Gona, Vera Harley, Margaret Kariuki, Ernestine Kiano, Alice Nkilote and Mary Suthren. There was no money budgeted for delegates' fares so the NGS approached East African Airways. They told her that they couldn't give reductions unless the group was 12 or more, it would then be regarded as a football team! So Vera telephoned Uganda YWCA and as they were sending 6 delegates, they agreed to come to Nairobi by train and leave with the 'Team' thus cutting the fares by 50 per cent.

The Conference was most instructive and greatly enjoyed by everyone, there being 78 delegates from 12 African countries.

On the Sunday morning, Vera and Margaret decided to worship at Salisbury Anglican Cathedral, which proved to be a unique experience for Margaret. The C.M.S. had brought the "low" church to Kenya but the U.M.C.A. had brought the "high" church to Rhodesia. When the acolyte entered, swinging the incense, Margaret whispered to Vera, "We've come to the wrong church". Vera whispered back that it was another form of the same church, and after the Service explained about the various missions. Margaret declared that she would tell her father, who it will be remembered, was a Bishop. He, no doubt, knew all about the various levels of Anglicanism.

The Kenya delegation to the YWCA's all-Africa Conference in Salisbury/Harare in 1961

Vera Harley was detailed to be responsible for the New Year's Eve programme. This resulted in a very successful Nativity Play, Maggie Gona playing one of the Shepherds. Mary Suthren returned with the group to Nairobi but Vera was asked to stay on for a conference on Education and to travel back with the World staff, seeing YWCA work en route. Whilst visiting Kitwe in the Copper Belt, she was introduced to someone connected with the mining industry who was interested to hear about the YWCA in Kenya. He offered the sum of £500 from a mining lottery. Vera thanked him but said that before accepting the money, she would have to consult the Chairman of Trustees. On returning to Nairobi, she explained all this to the Archbishop who was not agreeable to the YWCA accepting money from a lottery. When Vera Harley told the YMCA General Secretary he wrote to Kitwe and in due course received £500, which the YMCA Board said was to be used towards the building of a YM/YW Camp. Mr Jack Block offered for this purpose a 60 acre plot on the shores of Lake Naivasha.

According to the new Constitution, a Full Members' Convention was to be held annually. This was to begin with reports from all Local Associations and Groups, then a question and answer period, followed by leadership training sessions. The first of these took place at Limuru Conference Centre from 27-29th January. This was attended by the World President, Isabel Catto and Janet Thomson of World

Staff, both being on their way back from Salisbury. In order to encourage members around the country to participate, Executive agreed that every established group could send up to six delegates, H.Q. paying all expenses for the 2nd, 4th and 6th. This scheme worked satisfactorily, all groups being represented, usually by four members. The Convention was well supported and greatly enjoyed.

Meanwhile, the Mombasa Association was growing rapidly. There were two staff members but both were employed within the Hostel which was full and making a good profit but housing only European girls. Volunteers, still headed by Kitty Hall, were running Y-teen clubs for African girls, multiracial groups and educational classes. Maggie Gona, on returning from the YWCA All Africa Conference, was full of enthusiasm. She, and other African members, all had full-time jobs but they worked alongside Kitty and her team whenever they could find time and were taking increasing responsibility. Kitty Hall started a non-residential Vocational Training School in the Hostel much on the same lines as Nairobi. Just before Helen Haylett resigned as President, since she was leaving the country, the Mayor of Mombasa, appreciating the excellent work being carried out by the YWCA at the Coast, launched a very successful appeal on behalf of the Association.

At the March Executive meeting a report was given on the second Good Hostess Course which had lasted four weeks and had been attended by 14 clergy wives. This was an interesting ecumenical experience, for women came from villages within designedly separate Christian areas. The Kenya Missionary Council, later to become the Christian Council of Kenya had organised this denominational separation in order to spread their work, and prevent overlapping, agreeing upon the areas in which each should set up churches, schools,

After lunch at the first Annual Convention held at Limuru Conference Centre

teacher training colleges, hospitals etc. The C.M.S. being a Mission of the Church of England, known as Anglican, started work at the coast, in the Taita District, most of Nyanza, Fort Hall, Embu and part of Kiambu; the Presbyterian Church of East Africa was responsible for most of Kiambu District and ran a large mission at Tumu-Tumu. The Methodists worked at the coast and in Meru district and the Friends' African Mission in Kakamega District.

Relations between the different missionary societies was always good and the scheme worked well, resulting in the establishment of St. Paul's Theological College and the Alliance High School. But the arrangement did create geographical and, to some extent, tribal divisions, which meant that clergy wives had little opportunity of meeting their counterparts in other Christian traditions. Although accommodation was provided in St. Paul's compound for wives and families, it was not always economically practical for the women to be away from their shambas at seed time and harvest and in any case not all the students were married at the time of their training. The Good Hostess Courses gave these clergy wives a unique opportunity of living together in the YWCA and getting to know each other without the constraints of children. As a result there was much interest and discussion. At the Tea Party, on the last afternoon, husbands, of course, knew one another having formed ecumenical friendships at college and afterwards at C.C.K. meetings.

This had been followed by a two week Good Hostess Course for School Teachers.

The N.G.S. then read to Executive the official report received from World YWCA following Janet Thomson's visit. Weaknesses were listed as follows:
1. Lack of Y-teen work
2. Too little YWCA leadership training.
3. Too few African members on the Committees.

The Executive Committee's response to these criticisms was as follows:
1. Mary Suthren had established excellent Y-teen groups in several High Schools which Janet had not had time to see.
2. A Leadership Training Course was given every January as part of the Convention and the Trainees in the school were being instructed in YWCA principles on which they were tested.

Also Mary had organised YWCA courses in various parts of the country, not to mention the joint YM/YW courses which had been held.
3. Executive agreed that there were too few African women serving on committees. The main reason for this was that most urban African women were working, so could not attend meetings held in the morning, the time that suited European members, many of whom had served loyally for years. Committees outside Nairobi and Mombasa were almost entirely African.

Into the New Kenya — 1961

Bishop Trevor Huddleston visits the YWCA Vocational Training School

The report stated, however, that the Kenya Association appeared to be in the lead in Africa with regard to informal education, and the Vocational Training School was mentioned very favourably.

At the annual Women's World Day of Prayer, Nairobi members participated in the service held in All Saints Cathedral.

When the examination results of the first twelve Trainees arrived from London they were as follows:

London Council of Domestic Studies
Of the twelve students: all passed in needlework and dressmaking; all passed in homecraft, Lilian Njeri with first class honours.
The Homecraft examination included Hygiene, Laundry, Cookery, Catering and Nutrition.
The Royal Society of Arts English Examination for Foreigners
Five passed, Bilha Masida and Beth Njhira with credits.
The Red Cross Examination
Ten passed parts 1 and 2. This included Child Care, First Aid and Home Nursing.

The Trainees also took a paper on the history of the international work of the YWCA. A prize was given for the best paper.

One Sunday afternoon the Trainees had a very special visitor, the Bishop of Masasi the Rt. Rev. Trevor Huddleston. He was staying with the Provost of All Saints Cathedral, the Rev. Raymond Harries who kindly took him to see the YWCA and meet the students.

In April a very successful Parade of National Costumes was held in the International House lounge, many people from various High Commissions participating. This was organised, not only to raise funds for the Appeal but as part of the YWCA World Membership Day celebrations.

The charity "Bread for the World" of the German Council of Churches had sent £2,264 through World YWCA to be used for educational purposes, either towards the School Building or for future work. It will be remembered that the Executive Committee had decided in 1959 that educational work amongst African women should be the priority of the Association's programme. There were now eleven educational village groups and two in the townships of Nairobi.

Mrs. Edna Philbrick, wife of the Chaplain to Nairobi Hospital became Secretary and Personal Assistant to the N.G.S. and an "almost new" typewriter was purchased for £50.

The C.C.K. YM/YW Committee heard from Geneva that a staff member from the German YWCA would be arriving later in the year or early in the New Year to set up the Leadership Training Programme which had been proposed in 1960.

A monthly newsletter was now produced from Headquarters and was distributed free to every Branch.

Gwyneth Jackson told the Executive, at the June Meeting, that she had been offered a post by the YWCA in London and wished to leave Kenya on the 9th October.

In July, the Kenya Broadcasting Corporation allocated to the YWCA five minutes every other week on their Africa Programme, this to continue until January 1962. A radio sub-committee was therefore set up including Edna Collins as she was the only staff member who spoke Swahili.

The National Council met on 18th July 1961 and was chaired by the President, Lady Harragin. The Archbishop of East Africa gave the opening prayer. Over 70 people were present, delegates attending from all the Nairobi groups and hostels, including a newly formed group at King George VI Hospital. The Associations in Mombasa, Meru, Kisumu, Kitui, Kiambu and Nyeri were also represented. The guest of honour was Miss Janet Lacey C.B.E. She was accompanied by the Rev. Paul Feuter, General Secretary of the C.C.K. who urged that more African women should be elected to the Executive Committee. Mrs. Gecaga was a Vice-President and Mrs. Hannah Rubia and Mrs. Phoebe Asiyo were already serving. The Chairman assured the meeting that the Association was anxious to find more African members able to serve but educated African women were extremely busy and in great demand by all voluntary organisations.

Elections took place, including the addition to the Board of Trustees of Mr. Hugh Greenwood, who would represent the Association at the Coast.

In her Report the N.G.S. stated that the committee structure, implemented in 1960, was working well. The new Bridge Block, so called because it was the bridge between the old hostel and the new, had been built and furnished at the cost of £13,000, £2,264 having been generously donated by the German Charity "Bread for the World". The building comprised the School, with dormitories above for the 24 Trainees and on the top floor, 20 single rooms adjacent to International House. The new bedrooms were already occupied and the Trainees would be moving into their new premises at the end of the month. She said she knew how much they would appreciate the excellent domestic science equipment which had been installed in the School. Reporting on the Good Hostess Courses, she told Council that they were held regularly and always fully booked. Satisfactory reports had been received from all local associations and from Mombasa Branch, where a very good educational programme was functioning under the leadership of Kitty Hall. Work in High Schools and Teacher Training Colleges around the country continued to thrive; there were 80 Full Members at the A.G.H.S. Miss Harley concluded her report by thanking the Trustees, committee members and staff for their hard work, loyalty and support. The N.G.S.'s Report was well received, and in proposing its adoption the Archbishop thanked Miss Harley, wishing her a happy and restful leave, and saying that he knew that he voiced the feelings of the meeting when he said that he was glad she had agreed to return for a further term.

Lengthy discussion took place regarding the proposed loan by Nairobi City Council of Ofafa Hostel to the YWCA and the N.G.S., with the support of the Trustees, was asked to continue negotiations and to seek the necessary funds.

The joint YM/YW work was discussed and concern was expressed about the lack of leadership by women in these mixed groups. If this joint work was to continue, Council decided that equal opportunities and full partnership must be established.

The Chairman welcomed Janet Lacey and asked her to address Council. Miss Lacey said that it gave her great pleasure to be with the Kenya Association at their Annual Meeting, particularly as it was being held in the building for which, only 19 months previously, she had laid the Foundation Stone. She expressed her congratulations on the progress made since her last visit and wished the Association every success. She then presented certificates to the Trainees who had graduated from the Nairobi V.T.S. Votes of thanks followed and the Rev. Paul Feuter closed the meeting with prayer.

By 1961 a YM/YW group had been formed at Ruiru township. Whereas the group at the Sisal Estate were rural folk with little education, the township members comprised young men and women with at least eight years schooling, some with a good deal more. They invited Vera to be their speaker at a Sunday afternoon meeting. Being her week-end off, she spent Saturday night at the home of a Committee Member who lived near Ruiru. On Sunday morning her host and hostess took her to Ruiru Church with them. These rural churches, built by white

Vera visits the Day Nursery at Ngewa Village

settlers for themselves, were usually built of stone and of mock medieval architecture, making the worshippers feel very much at home.

After lunching with her friends, Vera set off for the meeting and was welcomed by the Chairman, who asked if she had been to church that morning. She pointed to the church where she had worshipped. "We're not allowed there" he observed, "so we have to use the Schoolroom". Vera queried this, but on reflection she realised that there had been no Africans in the Church, and it certainly was not a matter of language. Somehow she felt guilty, and promised to ask the Archbishop about it, which she subsequently did. He was saddened but not surprised, explaining that two Anglican Churches had been established in Kenya, an African and a European. He was "father" to them both, being the only link between the two communions. He prophesied that things would very soon change.

In 1961, the Red Cross suggested that the Trainees who had passed their examinations might like to form the first African Red Cross Group. Seven agreed to become members, and the first assignment they were given was to help out at Pumwani Maternity Hospital.

The YM/YW Hostel in Nakuru was now going well, accommodating eight men and six women; there was still room for six more residents. The Swedish couple Mr. and Mrs. Garvers were doing a splendid job.

The National President and the National General Secretary made a tour round Mount Kenya meeting groups at Tumutumu, Ngutu, Kiagonde, Nyeri, Nanyuki, Meru, and Kigare. Meru requested books for a library, Nyeri stressed the need for a YWCA hostel, and Nanyuki asked for a field worker.

Into the New Kenya — 1961

Gladys Beecher suggested that Vera should join her on a visit to a large meeting of the Mothers' Union in a rural church somewhere near Embu. Vera was asked to tell an assembled gathering about the YWCA of which they had never heard. It was Kikuyu country and as always Gladys translated impeccably. The first question to Vera was how many children had she. Gladys explained that, as she had never married Vera had no children. Much murmuring ensued; they were obviously very sorry for her. Gladys then asked if they would like to make Vera an honorary member of the Mothers' Union; to this they most heartily agreed. All these women would have had shambas and been able to feed their families with the produce but they said there were some commodities that they had to buy which were very expensive, such as sugar. When this was interpreted, Vera, remembering the large barrel shaped bee-hives which hung on many trees in the African reserves asked why they didn't give their families honey and this was translated. A pregnant silence ensued. "Oh dear," said Gladys, "we have shocked them. Honey is only used by the old men to make pombe which makes them drunk." Gladys decided that she must explain that honey was good and not evil and that the women should make sure that they had their share, for it was nutritious. She then described in great detail, how to filter and purify honey to make it ready for their children to eat. Let us hope that some of their children joined the YWCA.

Elizabeth Forbes and Jean Hollingsworth, the two V.S.O.s, were due to leave in September. They had done excellent work and were very popular with the Trainees. Soon Susan Higgett and Fiona (known as Fifi) arrived and began to work happily with staff and in the School.

A Good Hostess Course for the wives of army officers was successfully organised in October. The wife of the Commanding Officer had been to see the N.G.S. about this course and Vera was surprised when she said "My husband says it is essential that you teach them how to drink"! She went on to explain that most of these women had never seen a bar or been to a "Drinks" Party and very soon they would be exposed to both. This was all passed on to the Education and Training Committee and they gave one or two sessions on how to give a drinks party, explaining that soft as well as alcoholic drinks should be offered, showing them the amount of spirits to be used per portion and the appropriate soft drinks to go with them, what glasses to be used for beer, sherry, wine etc. Delicious fruit juices were being produced in Nairobi and the Committee wrote to the firm about this rather special Course. No doubt, realising that here was the possibility of a new market, generous quantities of various fruit juices were donated for the students to sample.

As mentioned at Council, the N.G.S. was due for home leave. It so happened that, by the end of September, Edna Collins, who had been seconded from the C.M.S., was also due for furlough. This meant that, of the senior staff, only Mary Suthren and Margaret Kariuki were left, but by now, there were several young members of staff trained in the V.T.S. taking responsibility for village work and working as assistant wardens and there was a full time secretary in National Office.

Because of the interest that the German YWCA and Churches were taking in the Kenya Association, World Office asked Vera to spend some time during her leave in that country. Before she left, a volunteer had very kindly made a short film showing some of the work being carried out by the Association. When Vera arrived in Geneva, a meeting of World Executive was in progress and members were keenly interested in all that was happening in Kenya. After some days there, Vera flew to Germany where she was given a warm welcome by Gertrud Friedrich and her staff. Vera gave several talks to YWCA groups of all ages, and showed the film, which was well received. She also spoke to several Church Groups. On every occasion a collection was taken so Vera left with £50 and the promise of a Minibus for educational work.

The N.G.S. then flew to Heathrow and before celebrating Christmas with her family, she spent several days in London with her old friend Jean Begg, now retired from the YWCA and living in New Zealand, J. B. was paying what was to be her last visit to Britain.

In November another Good Hostess Course was held in Nairobi for clergy wives when emphasis was on the ways in which they could assist their husbands in their parishes — how to organise women's groups, Sunday schools etc. This proved a very valuable course and was much appreciated.

The YM/YW Centre which opened in 1958 in Ngewa Village, was being well used. Francis, a young African man who lived nearby, started a pre-school play group, giving up all his time to this "Y" project. Every weekday, mothers left their children with him as they went to work in the fields and they would collect them at 3 p.m. Francis taught them their letters and numbers and many songs and games. A more delightful group of tiny children it would have been difficult to find, and all this was organised by one volunteer.

The Hostel Committee held a Christmas Fair in Windsor House which was very enjoyable and successful. Edna was back on duty by the beginning of December and assisted in creating the usual all Residents happy Christmas in Windsor House.

1962. Golden Jubilee

1962 was an important year for Nairobi as the first African Mayor, Councillor Mr Charles Rubia, was elected.

On 2nd January, Vera Harley started her journey back to Kenya, stopping off at Geneva where she was told about the All Africa Christian Youth Assembly which was to take place in Nairobi, in January 1963, under the auspices of the World Council of Churches, Student Christian Movement and World YMCA and World YWCA.

Into the New Kenya — 1962

Elizabeth Palmer, World General Secretary, showed Vera an American magazine which had a heading in large print "Kenya YWCA teaches African Women to Drink". Elizabeth Palmer was not amused and asked what it meant. Vera said that she had no idea who had spoken to the press about the Good Hostess Course for army officer's wives and she explained the situation.

On one occasion in 1961, when the National General Secretary was returning from a C.C.K. meeting at Limuru conference centre with the Archbishop, he driving his land rover, he had said how good it would be if the YWCA could have a small chapel. Vera agreed and suggested that as only the large "Pre-fab" was required for accommodation, perhaps the smaller one could be converted. The Archbishop liked this idea, saying that it was in exactly the right position, just inside the main gate. He went on to say that it should be dedicated to one of the minor women saints. Silence fell as they thought about this. Then Vera suggested that it should be the chapel of Martha and Mary because in the YWCA you often had to stir the soup with one hand, whilst preparing hostel prayers with the other. The Archbishop thought this would be the right name. Vera was very shocked and disappointed when, on returning from her leave in 1962, she saw that the building was no longer there. On making enquiries, she was told that it had been removed and given away by order of the Hostel Committee, their reason being that more space was needed for parking residents' cars. This was very short sighted as, within a few years, Vera knew that the hostels would be catering for girls who could not afford cars. Though very angry, she was thankful that the larger building was still standing to accommodate students taking short courses.

Mary Suthren, having completed her contract, sailed for home on 2nd January 1962. She had served for seven years and had done a remarkably good job, often under extremely difficult circumstances. When she arrived in 1954, there was no African participation in the YWCA. It was Mary who introduced the Association to African and Asian women and girls, and with patience, tact and perseverance created a multi-racial movement. Many African women, holding important posts in Kenya, had their first experience of committee structure and workings from Mary. It was now up to the young African women to carry on and expand the work Mary had initiated with such enthusiasm and foresight.

Soon after the N.G.S. 's return, the Annual Convention was held and well supported. Delegates from all parts of the country participated. The meetings were held in H.Q. Conference Room and the remaining pre-fab provided 12 beds towards the accommodation.

Whilst in London, the N.G.S. had, on the instruction of the Executive Committee, appointed a new Hostel Director. As she was not due to arrive until February, Eve Middleton, the very efficient Deputy Warden and her staff continued to take charge of International House. Edna Collins and Margaret

Scenes from the 1962 Annual Convention held at National HQ

Above: Delegates walking up to the School. The back of Beecher House can be seen on the right

Kariuki were busy with the School and Edna was also co-ordinating programme work at H.Q., in the townships and villages.

Miss Hildegarde Seidal, the staff member from the German YWCA promised to C.C.K./YM/YW committee had arrived and everyone was delighted to have her living in Beecher House whilst she organised her leadership training project.

Early in February, the Duke and Duchess of Gloucester, the Duke being Queen Elizabeth's uncle, visited Kenya and the Duchess agreed to go to the YWCA to see the School and the Good Hostess Course which was in progress. She must have been impressed with what she saw, for on the following day, a B.B.C. man arrived, having received instructions from London to take pictures for British television of YWCA educational work in Kenya.

At the February Executive meeting, the N.G.S. was able to report to the committee on her lecture tour of Germany and told them about the forthcoming All Africa Christian Youth Assembly, explaining that the Association would be heavily involved throughout the year in the preparation. Reporting on the School, Edna Collins said that there were over 100 names on the waiting list from all over East Africa. The Education and Training Committee had decided to raise the fees from shs 150 to shs 200 a year. A Good Hostess Course was in progress and five more were planned for the year. Edna had made a very successful broadcast about the work of the Association on the K.B.C. Swahili programme.

Into the New Kenya — 1962

Winifred Pole, the new Hostel Director, arrived on 26th February. For the first time, the hostels were to work as one unit. In order to be located between Beecher House and International House, she lived in what had been built as the Headmistress's flat in the School building: thus she was able to keep an eye on the Trainees and residents in both houses. Margaret Kariuki was still living in her accommodation in the school, whilst Edna moved to Mary's old flat in the National Block.

The Tea Room was going fairly well but was not making a steady profit. It was being run by one of the V.S.O.s and a graduate from the School.

One afternoon, early in the year, Mrs Tameno from Ngong, wife of an agricultural officer, called to see the N.G.S. about starting an Association. Ngong is a small township about ten miles from Nairobi situated on the lower slopes of the Ngong hills not far from where Karen Blixen, author of "Out of Africa", once lived. Mrs Gladys Beecher, wife of the Archbishop, happened to call at the same time and both had tea in the garden with Edna and Vera. Gladys recounted that Mrs Tameno's father was amongst the first of the Maasai tribe to be baptised. Mrs Tameno said that already she had a group of women, Christian and Muslim, wanting to join the YWCA and a date was made for the N.G.S. to visit them. The sun sets in Kenya about seven o'clock all the year round and, as time was getting on, Vera asked Mrs Tameno who would be driving her home. She replied that as her husband was on safari, she would have to catch a bus. Realising that it would be dark before the bus reached Ngong, Vera and Edna decided to drive her. On reaching the township, they said goodbye, but their passenger said that her house was about five miles up the hills. The road was now but a narrow track tunnelling through six foot high elephant grass and hyenas were darting across, dazzled by the headlights. Vera asked Mrs Tameno how she would have got home had she travelled by bus. "I would have walked," she replied. "But there's a lot of game about. "Wouldn't you have been nervous?" enquired Vera. "I am Maasai" was the reply. "Have you ever been walking and come across lions?" asked Vera. "Oh yes, but I pretend I don't see them and they pretend they don't see me!" Before long, a good branch was formed and Mrs Tameno was co-opted on to the Executive Committee. Soon they had organised classes in Swahili and English, also child care, cooking and nutrition, meeting in the School building after the children had left.

Agatha Mwakambo, an ex-Bahati resident, was being trained in International House to be Assistant Warden at the Mombasa Hostel. The Association there was going well. V.S.O. Jean Gurney was a great success, being popular with residents, staff and members. The Hostel had its first African resident and the committee were planning non-residential Good Hostess Courses in the Hostel. Beatrice Ezekial, who had graduated from the School in 1961, and whose home was at the coast, was appointed to assist with the educational programme. In April, the Branch held their A.G.M., which was chaired by Vice-President Mrs Kitty Hall;

the N.G.S. was the guest speaker. Lady Sarah Wright, nee Waldegrave, was elected President, which meant that she automatically became a national Vice-President. It is interesting to note that her maternal grandmother, Mrs Arthur Grenfell, was National President of the British YWCA in the 1940s and that a distant kinswoman, the Honourable Mrs Montagu Waldegrave, mentioned frequently earlier in this history, was the fourth and sixth World President, serving from 1914-1924 and from 1928-1930, being one of the only two women to serve twice as World President. The Kenya Association had reason to be very grateful to her for the interest she had shown in the early days, and the encouragement and support she had given to the infant Branch in Nairobi.

Alice Nkilote wrote reporting on the Meru branch. The play "Countess Catherine" had been produced and a profit of Shs.35 had been made. Half had been donated to the Famine Relief Fund and the other half to the new YM/YW library in Meru.

Early in the year, the Probation Service had telephoned to book accommodation for Isabel Apindi who was coming from Kisumu for a week's training in Nairobi. The account was to be sent to Probation Headquarters. The N.G.S. therefore reserved one of the best rooms in International House. As she had a late afternoon meeting, Vera left a note at Reception for Isabel, saying that she would be back at 6.30 and would join her for dinner in the Hostel. When Vera returned she was told that the letter had been handed to Miss Apindi, who had asked to be transferred to Beecher House, the lower income hostel. She found Isabel and over dinner in Beecher House, asked why she had changed the booking. Isabel explained that she knew no one in International House, but had several friends in Beecher House. Vera then explained to her that, the next time she came to Nairobi, it was her duty to the European residents to stay in International House, because most of them had never met an educated African woman. This, of course, had never occurred to Isabel. She laughed and gave her promise. Six months later, she was in Nairobi for a Probation Officers' Conference and, true to her word, accepted accommodation in International House, where Vera joined her for dinner. It was a cold August evening and a big log fire burned in the lounge. As they sat by the fire drinking their coffee, gradually the residents came up and asked to be introduced to the guest and they all sat chatting to Isabel. She had done these European girls a real service.

There were 30 residents at Bahati Hostel, which was being run efficiently and happily by Mr and Mrs Kabuki. But the City Council wanted the premises back for a Home for Vagrants and, as discussed by National Council in 1961, had offered the YWCA the large hostel, only a mile away from Bahati, at Ofafa. This had been built for men who were in the City looking for work. It had been open and staffed for a year, but there had been no applicants. The N.G.S., therefore, went to see the City Treasurer and, when he asked what rent the YWCA were prepared to pay,

Into the New Kenya — 1962

she reminded him that the corporation had been losing money for a year. After some discussion, it was agreed that the YWCA should have the use of the building rent free until a profit was made, taking possession on 1st May. The accommodation consisted of four large dormitories, but it was obvious that the Bahati residents who had enjoyed sharing a little house between two, were not going to be happy in dormitories. Money to develop the building was scarce so an Ofafa Fund was set up. A resident in International House, Pat Hepple, a qualified architect, offered her services free. She drew plans for partitioning two of the dormitories; the other two were to be kept for students. The kitchen facilities had been built to provide simple breakfasts only, so a good deal of additions and alterations were necessary if catering was to be done. There was a good warden's flat at the top of the building and a caretaker's flat controlling the back entrance. It was very sad having to break up the excellent Bahati community, which had been established for over six years; only about 25 per cent of the residents agreed to move to Ofafa, the main excuse being that they liked doing their own cooking.

Minutes of the Executive in May reported that Mrs Fraser-Leigh, N.G.S. elect of Sierra Leone YWCA was to spend six weeks with the Kenya Association for observation and training at the request of World YWCA. Everyone enjoyed her visit and when the time came for her to leave, Vera thought it would be fun if the senior staff took her out for a farewell dinner. She therefore booked a table at a restaurant in Karen, just outside Nairobi. Before ringing off, the receptionist said "You are, of course, all Europeans". When Vera replied that there would be two African ladies and three Europeans, she was told that only Europeans could be admitted. Instead, a table was booked at an Italian restaurant in the city and everyone had a very jolly evening. Although the word "Apartheid" was never mentioned in Kenya, racial discrimination certainly existed.

The N.G.S. heard that Lord Dulverton of the Dulverton Trust was in Nairobi and she was able to make contact and invited him to tea. Whilst showing him round the hostels and School, she told him about the work being carried out in Kenya. This resulted in the Trust sending a donation of £1000.

V.S.O.s made a tremendous contribution to the work both in Nairobi and Mombasa over the years 1959 to the end of 1965. There was, however, one unfortunate incident which should be mentioned, if only because it reveals the fact that neither the British Army nor the YWCA staff adequately briefed young people new to Kenya. Two V.S.O.s became friendly with two young British servicemen. One Sunday they called, at about 5.00 p.m., and suggested a drive. As was usual, the girls told Miss Collins that they were going out. By 10.30 p.m. they had not returned. Knowing that they had no key, Edna waited up but by midnight she was extremely anxious and in fact had no sleep at all. At 8.00 a.m. she went to the N.G.S.'s flat and shared her concern, suggesting that the police should be informed. Vera's advice was to wait until 9.00 a.m. and if by then there was no

Mrs Fraser Leigh, N.G.S. designate, Sierra Leone, with Edna Collins, Margaret Kariuki and Winifred Pole. The Vocational Training School is in the background

news, to ring the Christian Council of Kenya, the local organisation to which the V.S.O.s were responsible. At 8.45, the car arrived in the drive below the National Office and four very bedraggled and frightened young people climbed out. Feeling immensely relieved, Vera asked them to come up and tell her what had happened. They had driven up into the Ngong Hills and, on the way back, the car had broken down. They had spent some time unsuccessfully trying to make a repair, then realised that one of them would have to walk some five miles to Ngong township and find a garage to tow them down. As it was by now quite dark, wild animals were moving about, their eyes shining in the blackness. This, of course, scared the youngsters and they decided to sit tight until dawn. They had no torch and no water. Had Edna thought that they were thinking of driving up into the hills, she would have told them that 5 p.m. was too late to set out. At first light, two of them had walked to the township and found a garage and were duly towed down. Once the repair was made, they drove back to the YWCA, after which the two young men had to face their officer for being "Absent without Leave". Meanwhile it was difficult for the N.G.S. to know what action to take. The 24 African Trainees in the School, who were much the same age as the V.S.O.s,

Into the New Kenya — 1962

knew that if any of them had stayed out all night, according to the rules laid down by their parents, they would be sent home immediately. Of course, this situation was entirely different, but it was important that the episode should not be seen as racial discrimination. Vera therefore rang the C.C.K. and a meeting was called which was attended by the N.G.S., Edna and the two girls. It was agreed that some sort of token punishment would have to be administered and it was decided that for one month the V.S.O.s should report back by 6 p.m. This at least showed the Trainees that justice was being done.

The Chairman of the YMCA and their National General Secretary, both European, were convinced that to save money and to expand the work more rapidly, there should be a joint Association, all work coming under the heading "YMCA/YWCA of Kenya". Tremendous pressure was put on Vera and she took the matter to Executive Committee. They were very doubtful that it would be the right course to take. One morning in June, the Kikuyu Bishop, the Right Reverend Obediah Kariuki, Margaret's father, paid an unexpected call on Vera. She was surprised and delighted to see him. He told her that he had heard about the YMCA's idea and that he did not want this to happen. Vera told him that she was only waiting for some guidance on the matter, and thanked him for giving her this guidance. She asked the Bishop why he was so adamant. He replied that in a joint Movement, the men would do all the talking and the women would do all the work. He felt that, if a really strong YWCA were established, it would be an incentive to the men to build a strong YMCA. Vera asked him if he would very kindly put his ideas into a statement which could be read to the National Council in July. This he agreed to do.

In June, Gladys Beecher told the N.G.S. that the YWCA in Kenya was approaching its Golden Jubilee. She said that she remembered, as a little girl, being told by her aunt, Mrs Burns, a founder member of the Nairobi Branch that it had been started in 1912 and she remarked — "the original Minute Book must be somewhere." Repairs were taking place at that time in the vicinity of the staircase, and Eve Middleton miraculously found this precious old book under the stairs. Everyone was delighted and it was decided that as the actual birthday in February had already gone, the Golden Jubilee celebrations should be organised later in the year on a date convenient to the Patron, the Archbishop and the Executive Committee. Mrs Jean Ellison, a member of the Education and Training Committee, and a voluntary teacher in the School, offered to organise the next fork luncheon and make it "Golden". She managed to produce a delicious meal of saffron chicken and rice: in fact all the food was golden in colour. This unusual luncheon was greatly appreciated.

The Appeal had gone very well and the £5,000 borrowed from Inter-Church Aid was repaid to the C.C.K. The Girl Guides who had paid the YWCA £500 for a five-year lease of an office and a storeroom, were about to vacate the premises after only 2 1/2 years; £250 had therefore been refunded to them.

The hostels were full and it was noted that Beecher House kitchen, which had been designed for 30-40 residents was now catering for 90; this included the Trainees and Good Hostess students. Bulk buying for both Beecher and International houses had now been established.

As Margaret Kariuki was very capably running the School and Beecher House with the assistance of two V.S.O.s and the prefects, Edna went on a working safari to the Nyanza District. She addressed a group of 40 women at Butere and 25 at Maragoli where a YWCA was just beginning. At Kisumu she was warmly received by the local Branch and had enrolled 12 new Full Members. At Sariba T.T.C. she had spoken to a group of 70 women students. Unfortunately the Branch at Kisii had collapsed, but Mrs Ayodo, who would shortly be returning from a training course in Israel, felt sure that she would be able to revive it. Edna had met a thriving group of 30 members in Lumbwa, the Chairman being Mrs Lorna Francis, an ex-member of Mary Suthren's Whitehouse Road Branch. Lumbwa had built their own club room on a plot donated by the local church; there Edna had enrolled 12 Full Members.

At the Annual Meeting of the National Council on 10th July, 1962 the President, Lady Harrigan, was in the chair; the Archbishop opened the meeting with prayer. The President's opening remarks included congratulations to Mrs Rubia, a member of the Executive Committee who had recently become Mayoress of Nairobi. A message had been received from World YWCA which read "We are deeply appreciative of the wisdom and courage which the National Council has shown in the development of their work and wish them to know that all they are doing is a matter of deep interest to World YWCA and is carried in their prayers." Greetings and congratulations were received from Vice-Patron Mrs Bibby of Mombasa, enclosing a donation of Shs 2,000. Among other letters of congratulation for the Jubilee, was one from Miss Ethel Gem, whose name appeared again after 40 years. Now in her nineties, living in England, she wrote, very kindly sending a donation, saying that she had been the first Warden of the first Hostel in Nairobi. The last mention of her in this history was in 1922 when she had sailed to Jerusalem to take up an important post for World YWCA. It would have been interesting to know what had happened to her since then. As she knew about the Kenya Jubilee, she must have still been in touch with the Association in Great Britain.

Council was attended by over 80 people, including Dr Von Stackelberg, Consul-General of the West German Republic, and the Baroness Von Stackelberg. Several delegates came from Mombasa and District, from Kisumu, Kiambu and from all the branches in high schools, teacher training colleges and the Royal College. Elections took place and Mrs Margaret Gecau, Matron in Chief of Kenya and Mr John Kamau, General Secretary of the C.C.K., were elected to the Board of

Into the New Kenya — 1962

Trustees. Five new African members were elected to the Executive Committee, being Mrs Adu, Mrs Perpetua Kaigwa, Mrs Kinya, Mrs Tameno and Mrs Deborah Otuga. A new Standing Committee was set up to represent YM/YW groups and much discussion took place regarding this work. Concern was expressed about the lack of female leadership, especially in the Kiambu District. A statement was read from Bishop Kariuki of Fort Hall, saying that he was not in favour of joint Associations. He advocated that the YMCA should be run by young men and the YWCA by young women, and he went on to say that he felt sure that joint Associations would not encourage women to stand on their own feet. He was, however, in favour of the two Associations coming together for religious and social activities. Mrs Kariuki then spoke in Kikuyu, endorsing her husband's statement, which Mrs Beecher kindly interpreted. The N.G.S. said that the new YM/YW Standing Committee would take note of the opinions expressed by Council and would report regularly to Executive. It was agreed that the matter would be reviewed by Council in 1963.

In her report, the N.G.S. said that the hostels were full and the Appeal had been very successful. The City Council hostel at Ofafa had been taken over by the Association on 1st May. Funds permitting, it was hoped that the new centre would be opening in November. Educational work had been greatly extended both in Nairobi and Mombasa. With the arrival of Miss Seidal from Germany, whom she welcomed, leadership training would doubtless increase. There were now 18 YWCA educational programmes operating in the Kiambu area. She pointed out that there were still immense opportunities in the field of education, staff and finance permitting. The School was running very successfully, as were the Good Hostess courses.

Speaking of the Government's request for accommodation for their Trainees she said that little was available, but that schemes for providing uniform accommodation specifically for Government Trainees were being explored. She had suggested to the authorities that the problem might best be solved by adding another floor to Beecher House. She welcomed Miss Pole, the newly appointed Director of Nairobi Hostels, Mrs Catherine Mbathi, General Secretary Eastlands and her assistant, Miss Rhoda Nyoka. She paid tribute to Mary Suthren, who had left for England in January.

Referring to her own long leave, she mentioned her visit to Geneva, both on her way to and from England, and spoke about her lecture tour in Germany. She said that during Miss Collin's furlough, World YWCA had arranged for her to see several National Associations on her way back to Kenya. Miss Collins had now taken over the organisation of Miss Suthren's work, employing young African staff trained in the YWCA School. In conclusion, she announced that the Association in Nairobi was now 50 years old and that the Golden Jubilee would be celebrated in October. The Report was adopted by Mrs Rubia, who proposed a

Rickshaws to Jets

vote of thanks to the N.G.S. This was seconded by Mrs Timmis. The Chairman then called upon Mrs Margaret Gecau to present certificates to the Trainees who had graduated in 1961. The Archbishop closed the meeting with prayer.

Late one afternoon, Edna Collins bounded into the N.G.S. 's office, obviously very angry. A young man had called to see her, having come straight from his office, saying "I've impregnated one of your Trainees." Edna had told him, in no uncertain terms, that he should be ashamed of himself and demanded that he should ask his employer for Friday off so that she could drive him with Trainee Winnie back to her village. Although Vera doubted that he would have the courage to face Edna's wrath again, he duly arrived and taking with her Susan, an excellent V.S.O., Edna and the young lovers set forth with sandwiches, water and a torch. It was not an easy journey, it meant driving 224 miles down the Mombasa road to Voi, then turning right into the Taita Hills. Eventually, they reached Winnie's village. Fortunately, both parents were at home, but neither spoke English. As Edna didn't speak Taita, they managed to communicate in Swahili and it was not long before Edna realised that she and the YWCA were being blamed for the whole situation. Leaving the young man with the family, Edna and Susan started the journey back. Before they reached the Mombasa road, it was lighting up time and they noticed that all the traffic bound for Mombasa was stationary. They then found themselves driving through what appeared to be a forest of huge tree trunks which neither of them remembered seeing on their outward journey. Suddenly they realised that they were among a great herd of elephants, the "tree trunks" being the elephants' legs. It was no use stopping, so Edna continued to drive and when they reached the main road and turned left for Nairobi, the last of the herd was still crossing, holding up all the traffic. Heads came out of the still stationary cars, to have a look at the mad person who had driven through the herd of elephants. Feeling rather shaken, Edna decided to break the journey and they spent the night at Hunter's Lodge and she telephoned Vera from there. They arrived back safely the following day. The story has a happy ending. Winnie married her young man and they lived in a flat in Nairobi. Six months later, a beautiful baby daughter was born. Edna kept in touch with this young family for many years.

V.S.O. Susan Higgett and Fifi left in August and were replaced by Sally Dean and Patience Clatworthy; both proved to be excellent V.S.O.s Patience, being a Ranger, started a YWCA Ranger company.

In September, Mrs Tameno reported to Executive that her group was going well, but they were still looking for land on which to build. The Presbyterian Church had offered them a plot free of charge which she had declined as she knew it was important for the YWCA to be seen as ecumenical. She had hopes, however, of being given land by the local town council; that would make it much easier for Muslim women to attend. It will be remembered that in 1913 a similar

Into the New Kenya — 1962

situation was recorded.

On Friday 5th October, the Golden Jubilee was celebrated and, with the guidance of the Provost of All Saints' Cathedral, the Reverend Raymond Harries, a very beautiful service was prepared. Well before 4 p.m., All Saints Cathedral was full, coachloads of members having arrived from Machakos Teacher Training College and High School, from the African Girls High School, Kambui Teacher Training College and Kikuyu villages. Other members came by train from Mombasa, Kisumu and by bus from Meru. The processions formed in the porch outside the West door, the first being clergy of all races and denominations leading in the Archbishop. The YWCA procession was led by a Trainee called Mary Wanjiru, chosen for her excellent deportment, who carried a large blue triangle, which was accepted by the Archbishop and placed on the Altar for the duration of the Service. Mary was followed by the Patron, Lady Renison, walking with the National President, Lady Harragin. Next came the Senior Vice-President, Mrs Beecher, with Mrs Hannah Rubia, Mayoress of Nairobi and a member of Executive. Then followed Vice-Presidents, the Honourable Mrs Gecaga with Miss Miriam Janisch and finally the President elect, Mrs Kiano, with the National General Secretary. The Archbishop gave the address and prayers were offered for the YWCA, members dedicating themselves to work for the women and girls of Kenya, praying that the Association would be given the necessary guidance, resources, vision and courage to meet the challenges ahead. The Service over, a fleet of cars, buses and lorries carried over 400 guests to Government House where the Governor and Lady Renison gave a wonderful Reception. A week later, the N.G.S. called to thank Lady Renison and was told that Sir Patrick had enjoyed the YWCA party more than any since his arrival in Kenya; never before had he met so many charming young African women and girls. It certainly was a memorable occasion. Sir Patrick retired in November and Lady Renison wrote the following letter to the National President:

Government House

Kenya

East Africa

November 24th, 1962

Dear Lady Harrigan,

Thank you very much for your kind letter and good wishes.

It was nice of you to write and it is very warming to both of us that you feel the way you do.

We shall all be very sad indeed to leave Kenya. It will always be much in our thoughts and we shall always be wishing it well. It is such a lovely country and has so many good and nice people in it that it surely must in time become the happy place it should be.

I will write to the YWCA to resign my "Patronship". I am filled with admiration for the work the "Y" is doing here (as in the many places we have been) but here most of all. I think it has been so wise and so alive to the changing times and that it is making one of the biggest (if not "The biggest") contribution of any Social Welfare organisation to the welfare and emergence of women in Kenya. I feel I have played a very passive role here as Patron but I am glad to have been able to help in a very small way.

With very many thanks.

Yours sincerely,

Eleanor Renison.

The need for a YM/YW residence in Nakuru was short-lived for in October it closed down. This was disappointing for it had been hoped to stimulate the work in that area.

A very successful Christmas market was held on 2nd November, using the main lounge and under the verandah of International House.

The Ofafa Centre was opened on 1st December by the Mayoress, Mrs Hannah Rubia. Edna moved into the Warden's flat, taking with her Esther Wairumu, a Trainee who had qualified in 1960 since when she had held two quite responsible jobs. Before long, the place was three-quarters full; Esther moved into the Warden's flat and Edna back to Headquarters. Esther was the first girl trained in the YWCA School to become a Hostel Warden and she did an excellent job for which she was later rewarded. There was lots of space at Ofafa and enormous potential. The urgent need was for a Day Nursery to assist working mothers in that part of the City, so Vera wrote to Geneva and asked for the assistance of trained staff. In the meantime, however, Edna Collins with the help of two Trainees who had graduated in 1961, opened a small Day Nursery under the guidance of the staff of the Lady Northey Home. Soon, an offer of help came from the Presbyterian Women of the U.S.A. who sent money to equip the Day Nursery and promised to send a qualified worker within a year. An offer of another qualified worker came from the YWCA of Japan and funds for teaching nutrition came from Australian Inter-Church Aid. The next task was to find funds with which to equip a Commercial School which could be residential as there was still room in one of the dormitories. African parents who did not live in the City were loath to let their daughters take up any training in Nairobi unless safe accommodation was provided. Gradually money came in and typing and English classes were set up. It was realised that schoolgirls whose parents lived nearby, usually in very crowded conditions, had difficulty in doing their homework, so a Homework Club was formed and girls went direct from school to the Centre to complete their homework before going home. Hannah Rubia, although busy with her duties as Mayoress, still found time to serve on Executive and Ofafa committees. Mrs Kaigwa, later to become a National President, was now Chairman of

Into the New Kenya — 1963

Ofafa and, together with Mrs Rubia, she started this new piece of work and continued to keep a keen and vigilant interest.

The time had come again to find jobs for the Trainees who were due to leave the school in January. Fortunately all of them obtained interesting posts. Miss Giles, the Senior Cookery Demonstrator for the E.A.P.&L. who had been giving weekly lessons to the Trainees ever since the School building was opened in 1961 was so impressed by the standard achieved that she chose one of them, Mary Wanjiru, to join her staff as a Trainee Demonstrator. Five years later, Mary was to be seen on television demonstrating cooking on the Swahili programme.

The dinner on Christmas Day for all residents was now well established. This Christmas was special because the Reverend Michael Mansbridge, Chaplain of the Royal College, and his wife Fiona joined the party with their three months old son in his Moses basket. As always, the Domestic Staff entered into the spirit of the occasion.

1963. World YWCA Council in Denmark

Because of the World YWCA's interest in launching the All Africa Christian Youth Assembly, the N.G.S. had been heavily involved throughout 1962 with the committee preparing for this important event. The Kenya Association was to be responsible for accommodating all the female delegates (approximately 200), 20 of whom were YWCA members in their own countries. This mammoth task was carried out very efficiently by Winifred Pole. As the Assembly was to take place during the Christmas vacation, the Women's Halls of Residence at the Royal College were available and came under her care. A few girls were, however, found beds in the YWCA. including the delegates from Ethiopia. They asked why there was no Association in their country. Janet Thomson was World YWCA's representative at the Assembly so this news soon reached Geneva and, before long, plans were afoot to set up an Association in Addis Ababa

Almost 500 young people, from almost every country in Africa, attended the Assembly, which met in the beautiful campus of Nairobi Royal College. The setting of the Assembly and the attire of the delegates in National Dress provided an ever present dramatically colourful illustration of the meeting of the old and new in Africa. Never could one lose sight of the Assembly Theme for, suspended squarely in the middle front of the stage in the Great Hall, was a three dimensional, six foot map of Africa on which was imposed a solid cross, under which was set out "Freedom under the Cross for Christians in Africa." It was indeed a vocal conference: always there were many more people waving hands wanting to speak than time ever permitted. There was some uneasiness, mainly from West African delegates because Christianity had arrived with the colonial system, but the Ethiopians soon put paid to that theory, declaring that they had embraced the Gospel hundreds of years before it was ever preached in Europe. This was amazing news to many people present and, because of its importance, a telephone call was made to Addis Ababa which resulted in priests and acolytes, with all the sacred paraphernalia, being flown to Nairobi, thus enabling a wonderful colourful Eucharist to be held in the ancient tradition of the Ethiopian church. The fact that Christianity had been accepted in Africa before Europe seemed to give a boost of confidence to the young people present. Discussions were honest; delegates coming together in Christian love felt free to talk about matters that were of real importance to them. Politics were, of course, discussed, for Independence was burning in all their young hearts. The raison d'etre of the Assembly was to help young Africans to use their new-found freedom with discipline and stewardship. Summing up, Dr Visser t'Hooft, General Secretary of the World Council of Churches, urged delegates to believe that "wherever the Gospel is proclaimed, it will finally do its work of energising, exploding and transforming life."

At the end of the Assembly, the YWCA was asked to give the V.I.P. luncheon for 80 guests. Mrs. Kanta Patel, an Indian member of the Executive Committee, very generously offered to provide and organise this. Assisted by the senior Trainees, she prepared a delicious buffet lunch in Beecher House. The N.G.S. asked the Russian Bishop, who was one of the delegates to say Grace in his own language and later she introduced him to the Matron-in-Chief of Kenya. The Matron was amazed and said: "You are Russian and a Christian?" "Yes," said the Bishop, holding up the cross which hung round his neck. "Well," said the African lady, "that just shows what lies we are told." The Bishop smiled and said that everyone must beware of propaganda. The women of his Church had asked him to present a gift to a leading African woman and, with great dignity, he handed her a beautifully carved casket.

As with the All Africa YWCA Conference in Salisbury, this Assembly enabled members from many different countries in Africa to meet. It was a very hectic, exciting and rewarding experience.

Immediately following the Assembly, the YWCA Annual Convention was held at the Kenya High School, being the first occasion on which Africans had been accommodated there. This was partly a World YWCA, and partly a Kenya meeting for, not only were two members of World staff present, but also 20 members from different countries in Africa who had attended the Assembly, including Mrs. Nyerere, wife of the President of Tanganyika, and Mrs. Obote, wife of the President of Uganda. The Kenya Association was well represented and for many members it was their first opportunity to experience the YWCA as an international movement. Mrs. Gecaga was Chairman of the Convention. On the first day, Mrs. Adu chaired the meetings, on the second, Mrs. Ernestine Kiano and, on the third, Mrs. Pamela Mboya. Mrs. Rubia, Mayoress of Nairobi, kindly invited everyone for Tea at the City Hall on the last afternoon. This was a very happy party and an enjoyable way of concluding an unusual Annual Convention.

Into the New Kenya — 1963

Delegates to the 1963 Annual Convention held at Kenya High School — the first occasion Africans were accommodated there

1963 continued to be a busy year, with Hostels full and the School going from strength to strength. Good Hostess Courses continued to be very popular. Educational classes were running successfully at Ofafa where the Day Nursery was serving an important need.

Independence was looming and suppressed excitement could be felt amongst the young people in the villages. But these folk were mission trained and as Jocelyn Murray explains in her book 'Proclaim the Good News', missionary leaders had shown great concern for education, some concern for social problems but little concern in encouraging African Christians in political action. Rural Africans were naturally polite and were apt to give the answer which they thought one would like to hear, so when asked if they were interested in politics they always said "No." The YMCA and YWCA leaders told them that as Christians they should take part in building up the new Kenya using their influence for good, They seemed surprised that Europeans should be encouraging them to think politically and to be assuring them that it was their Christian duty to do so. In 1960, African Church leaders, realising how important this was going to be for independent Kenya, had organised a conference at Limuru Conference Centre which was attended by leading African politicians.

Edith Wanjiru, a graduate from the School, was invited by Miss Rae Bowman, Principal of Kiambu Teacher Training College, to live at the College free of charge so that she could walk daily to the nearby YM/YW centre at Ngewe to work with women and girls there. Her salary was paid by Headquarters out of a grant by World YWCA for African staff.

Rickshaws to Jets

In a letter to Elizabeth Palmer dated 1963, Vera says, "At last the YMCA General Secretary has admitted to the Archbishop that unless YM/YW members join the two Movements separately, knowing what they are doing and paying subscriptions, nothing useful will be achieved." This was more or less what Mary Suthren had said in 1959. There can be no doubt, however, that something of lasting value was achieved as exemplified by the Provost of All Saints' Cathedral.

Mrs. Middleton, the Assistant Warden in International House, who had served so well since 1957 returned to England in March and Mrs. Venn, the Housekeeper, became Deputy Warden. Two Trainees who had graduated from the School joined the staff as Housekeeper and Receptionist.

It was in March also that the N.G.S.' Personal Assistant, Mrs. Edna Philbrick, affectionately known as 'Pill', became unwell and before she was fit to return to work, her husband had been appointed Dean of Mombasa. Mrs. Pettit took over from her, unfortunately only temporarily as she was shortly sailing for India.

In March, Mrs. Rockefeller of the American YWCA visited Nairobi and called on the N.G.S. She took a keen interest in everything she saw. This resulted in her giving a donation of £1,000.

At the request of World YWCA, the Kenya Association was pleased to welcome Miss E. Kamalao, secretary of the YWCA of Bulawayo for a period of observation.

Lady Harrigen told the Executive in June that she would be retiring from the Presidency at the Council Meeting in July. She felt that somebody younger and of the country should take over. Executive decided to propose to Council that Mrs. Kiano become National President. At the same meeting, the N.G.S. said that, with Independence coming to Kenya in December, she thought that the time had come for an African woman to replace her.

National Council took place on 7th July 1963 and was well attended. Lady Harrigen was in the Chair and she called upon Dr R.G.M. Calderwood, acting General Secretary of the C.C.K., to open the Council with prayer. Lady Harrigen said that it was the first Annual Council at which Archbishop and Mrs. Beecher had not been present. They were on their way to Toronto. She knew that everyone would send them best wishes, coupled with thanks for all they were doing for the Kenya Association.

Elections took place, Lady Harrigen became a Patron and Mrs. Ernestine Kiano was elected President. Three National Vice-Presidents were elected: Mrs. Beecher, Mrs. Gecaga and Mrs. Obel, née Isabel Apindi. Mrs. Hannah Rubia was elected World Council delegate. Mrs. Kiano then took over the chair. The usual Standing Committees were confirmed, the Eastlands and Ofafa Committees joining to become the Standing Committee for African Estates. Two new Standing Committees were formed for Finance and Personnel. It was decided that the Programme and Membership Committee should be replaced by a Membership Committee. The terms of reference were as follows: preparation of all programme material for members, including World Membership Day, Week of Prayer, Convention, and Training for Full Membership. It was explained that the General Programme of the Association for Members and non-Members was being carried out by the various committees. Chairmen were elected to each of the new committees. Elizabeth Normand said she would shortly be leaving Kenya and tendered her resignation. The Chairman said that the Education and Training Committee had done a splendid job since its inception in 1959 and expressed congratulations and sincere thanks to Mrs. Normand. Mrs Anne Booth-Clibborn was elected to take over from her. Thanks were also expressed to Mrs. Eve Ross, who had recently left the country. Not only had she been a very efficient Chairman of the Hostels Committee, but had given valuable assistance as a member of the Education and Training. Elections to the Executive Committee resulted in the number of European and African Members being equal, so things were improving.

It was proposed by the African Girls' High School Branch and seconded by Mombasa, that the annual capitation fee for Full and Associate members whether YWCA or YM./YW should be two shillings a year, 75 cents of which would be sent to World Headquarters, the remaining shs 1.25 to be retained by National. Local branches should decide upon their own subscriptions.

Ofafa Centre was going extremely well and the appointment of Mrs. Julia Kituri as Day Nursery Supervisor was ratified. In her Report, the National General Secretary said that seven Good Hostess Courses had taken place over the year for School teachers, for the wives of clergy, army officers, government officials, and civil servants and one for the wives of leaders in industry. A very encouraging report was received from Mombasa branch where Karen Johnson was a splendid V.S.O., giving valuable assistance with the Educational Programme; they would be sorry to lose her in August. The Hostels were all full, International House had really earned its new name, having accommodated guests from 20 different countries. There were now 146 beds in the compound, fees ranging from shs 180 to shs 480 per month. She proposed that, on returning from leave, she should become Advisory Secretary and that funds be sought to provide the salary for an in-training N.G.S. Thanking Lady Harrigen, she said what a hard working and supportive President she had been. She also expressed thanks to the Trustees, officers, committee members and to her colleagues on the staff.

Closing the meeting, Mrs. Kiano thanked everyone for attending and gave a vote of thanks to the N.G.S. She then reminded delegates that there would be a corporate Communion at All Saints' Cathedral the following morning which she hoped they would attend. Dr Calderwood closed the Council with prayer.

On 12th July, Mrs. Louise Leber from the U.S.A. and on 14th, Miss Minami from the YWCA of Japan, both Child Care Instructors, arrived to supervise the Day

Nursery Training programme at Ofafa. Immediately, students of eight years education were accepted for a two year training course in the subject.

In August, Mrs. Kiano told the N.G.S. that a group of African women were about to leave for America to attend a training seminar and that Mrs. Margaret Mugo was to be one of them. Mrs. Kiano and Vera unofficially asked Margaret if she would consider joining the staff on her return in December to train as N.G.S. Ernestine Kiano knew Margaret well and Vera had met her on several occasions at various meetings in Nairobi, but as she lived in Naivasha, where there was no YWCA, she had not become a Member. Margaret very sensibly asked for time to think about this proposal. Fortunately, just before leaving Kenya, she agreed. Vera then contacted World YWCA and they alerted the Association in America. This resulted in Margaret being given some initial training.

From 9th August to 21st, the first YM/YW work camp took place on the shores of Lake Naivasha. The leaders were Larry Millar, YMCA. and Prisca Ntui, YWCA Chairman Machakos Teacher Training College. Young people from Kenya and from several other African countries, also from Britain and America, participated. One evening the N.G.S. drove to Naivasha and joined in a very jolly group singing round the camp fire, the Kenyans teaching the others songs which had been composed to celebrate the forthcoming Independence.

The V.S.O.s had done an excellent year's work and were due to return to England, but neither Sally nor Patience wanted to leave Kenya. Once Vera was assured that their parents were agreeable, permission was obtained from V.S.O. Headquarters for their return passages to be postponed. Patience was a good typist and had occasionally helped out in National Office. When Mrs. Pettit left for India, Patience offered to take over the secretarial work until mid-November. Her offer was gladly accepted. Sally wanted to work at the Coast and the Association in Mombasa was only too pleased to welcome her. Whilst there, she met the son of a European farmer from Molo and became engaged. After marrying in England, they returned to Kenya to live.

Vera was not due for long leave until September 1964, but as she was to be part of the Kenya delegation at World Council in Denmark from 28th September to 11th October, Executive decided she should take her leave whilst in Europe. The National President asked her to be back in time for Kenya Independence celebrations in December. She therefore left for London with the elected delegate, Mrs. Hannah Rubia on 11th September, had two weeks' leave in England and flew with Mrs. Rubia to Denmark on 25th September where they met up with the National President, Ernestine Kiano.

This was a very special Council Meeting, for Kenya was upgraded from Category C to Category B. Before recommending this promotion, World Executive had taken into consideration the following: the Kenya Association had been affiliated to World YWCA for 45 years; it was inter-racial; there were 21 local

Into the New Kenya — 1963

At the World Council in Denmark (left to right) Elizabeth Palmer, World General Secretary, Isabel Catto, World President, Hannah Rubia, Council Delegate for Kenya YWCA, Vera Harley, N.G.S., Kenya

Associations and many YM/YW groups, there was a total of 338 Full Members, including some Roman Catholics; there were 1223 Associate Members, including Muslims, Hindus and Parsees; there was Hostel accommodation; frequent educational and training courses took place; affiliation fees of £20 were paid annually to World YWCA.

Vera was very anxious to enquire from American delegates about Margaret Mugo's progress. She was assured that Margaret was not only popular with her new friends in the U.S.A. but was an excellent student, thoroughly enjoying and making the most of the training and experience being given to her. Before leaving Denmark, World YWCA agreed with Vera that Margaret Mugo should return to Kenya via London where she would be given more training, thence to Geneva to visit World Headquarters and on to the Association in Athens for further experience.

Edna Collins and Hildegard Seidel, with the help of the Membership Committee, organised a programme for the Week of Prayer and World Fellowship in November. The YMCA regretted that they were unable to join in but promised to cooperate in 1964.

Soon after Vera left for Europe, Miss Pole became ill. By mid-November it was realised that her condition was very serious and a cable was sent to the N.G.S. by

Rickshaws to Jets

Dr Mary Miller, now Chairman of Hostels requesting her to return as soon as possible. Vera called at YWCA Headquarters in London and most fortunately met Doreen Boedeker who was on a visit from Kenya with the intention of spending Christmas with her brother and sister. On hearing about the crisis at the Nairobi Hostels, Doreen said that if necessary she would be prepared to curtail her holiday and return to assist Vera and the diminished staff.

The N.G.S. returned to Nairobi on 29th November to find the Christmas Market in progress in Beecher House. Mrs. Eva Thomson, a member of the Appeals and Publicity Committee, was in charge of this event which was very successful, raising over K.shs 16,000. Miss Pole was critically ill in hospital and Edna Collins, quite exhausted, was trying to hold the Association together. V.S.O. Patricia Clatworthy had only recently left for England. She had looked after the National Office very efficiently and the N.G.S. was relieved to find everything in excellent order. Only one V.S.O. had been allocated to Nairobi for 1963/64 and she had arrived after the N.G.S. had left for Europe. By the time Vera returned, she had decided that she would prefer to work for the Salvation Army and had made arrangements to transfer. However, the V.S.O. at Mombasa, Monica Murphy, had fitted in well and was doing excellent work.

Uhuru (Independence) was about to take place on 12th December 1963 and, as part of the celebrations, the YWCA had arranged a parade of national costumes and dances in Beecher House garden which was attended by over 300 people. Also Edna and Margaret set up three exhibitions of work done by the Trainees, at the School and at two other venues in the city. The Trainees were delighted to participate in the National Youth Rally in Nairobi. The N.G.S. was invited to represent the Association at all the functions associated with the Independence celebrations. Edna Collins decided to spend Uhuru Day with the girls at Ofafa, and she remembers going on the roof with them after dark and watching the light being carried up Mt. Kenya by the celebration team of the Mountain Club of Kenya, and at midnight seeing the bonfire lit on Peak Nelion, giving the signal for fires to be lit throughout the country.

At the same time, Vera was in the Arena sitting in the stand which was next to the one occupied by His Excellency, President Kenyatta, and the Duke of Edinburgh. She remembered seeing the Duke say something to the President just before midnight which made him roar with laughter. Some weeks later she learnt that the Duke had said: "Two minutes to go. You're sure you don't want to change your mind!" The hour of midnight was a very poignant moment, and everyone in that huge arena seemed to hold their breath as the Union Jack was lowered and the beautiful Kenya flag was hoisted.

On 15th December, Mrs. Catherine Mbathi organised the annual YWCA carol evening in International House lounge. Residents from all Nairobi Hostels attended, bringing their friends, and it was a very happy occasion. This was one of

Into the New Kenya — 1963

Catherine's last duties as a member of staff, because the Ofafa committee had decided that the staffing structure needed to be completely re-organised and that a resident director was necessary. Miss Pole's health was deteriorating and it was obvious that she would never again be well enough to take up her duties as Director of Hostels. Although every effort was made to find a replacement, this proved to be impossible. Vera therefore cabled Doreen Boedeker who, true to her word, returned to Kenya on the first possible plane, arriving a few days before Christmas and taking up her duties as temporary Warden of International House. It was, indeed, a great relief to have her back as she knew the Hostel so well and was a tremendous help during the festive season. Fifty people sat down for midday Christmas dinner, being residents and their friends from all the Nairobi Hostels.

News of Miss Pole's condition was now very serious and on Boxing Day she died. This caused great sadness as she was dearly loved by all the staff. Her funeral service took place on 27th December, over 100 people attending, the pall bearers being the African men on the Hostel staff. The University Chaplain, the Revered Michael Mansbridge, took the Service and spoke of the tremendous contribution which Miss Pole had made only a year before, in organising the sleeping accommodation for the woman delegates at the All Africa Christian Youth Assembly. The N.G.S. said "Winifred Pole will be remembered for the unity she brought about between the old Hostel and Beecher House, a unity which she established so resolutely and firmly that it is now and I hope always will be, taken for granted."

Advertisements were still in the National press for a Hostel Director. Several people were interviewed but no appointment was made. The whole place was running smoothly, however, with Doreen Boedeker in charge of International House and Margaret Kariuki at Beecher House. Edna Collins was keeping an eye on the School and Ofafa Hostel and co-ordinating the field and programme work. Margaret was now engaged to be married and, therefore, gave a month's notice. The Association offered her the post of Director, Ofafa, with married quarters, which she declined. Being the first African to hold a senior staff position, both committee members and staff were extremely sorry to lose her. She had certainly done a splendid job and made a valuable contribution to Beecher House and the School. Vera invited her and her fiance to dinner and promised to attend their wedding which was to be taken by the Archbishop early in the New Year.

Some kind friend presented the YWCA with its first television set. This was placed in the Conference Room thus making it available to residents of both hostels and to the Trainees.

1964. The first African National General Secretary

On 3rd, 4th and 5th of January, 1964 the Annual Convention was held in the Conference Room with accommodation in the pre-fab for members coming from long distances. Unlike previous years, only fifteen of the expected fifty residential

Vera Harley hands over to Margaret Mugo. July 1964

delegates arrived. The Meeting was to have taken place again at the Kenya High School; they were very understanding and allowed the booking to be cancelled without payment. With the tremendous celebrations of Independence just over, it was optimistic to hope that Convention would be as well attended as usual. On the Saturday some Branches and Groups were represented and several individual members came for the day, including a new member Mrs. Margaret Mugu, recently returned to Kenya. Vera was delighted to see her and told her the date of the January Executive Meeting to which she was to be invited. An excellent programme had been organised by Mrs. Gloria Hagberg of the Membership Committee and her efforts were not wasted for on Sunday morning the Conference room was packed to capacity. The National President, Mrs. Gecaga, chaired a panel of prominent women entitled 'Wanawake na Harambee', which, translated, means "women pulling together" On the panel were Mrs. Habwe, Mrs. Koinange, Mrs. Muthoni Likimani and Mrs. Pamela Mboya. A lively meeting ensued with many questions and answers, discussions, arguments and laughter. Summing up the Chairman said "Don't worry, we need the YWCA; it's the only place where we African women meet these days and don't quarrel."

Into the New Kenya — 1964

Once the Convention was over, a Good Hostess Course for the wives of Army Officers and N. C. O. s was arranged. This lasted four weeks and was attended by twelve resident students. On 20th January Archbishop and Mrs. Beecher again very kindly offered the hospitality of their home and chapel for a Retreat to which all committee members and staff were invited. This lasted all day so that every staff member was able to attend for part of the time.

When the Trainees' examination results arrived from the London Council for Domestic Studies, they were better than ever, and again the best in Kenya, all twelve students having passed — four with first class honours.

Rosemary Kairu, ex-chairman of the Y-Teens at the African Girls' High School, having passed her School Certificate, joined the YWCA staff taking over Margaret Kariuki's duties. In a letter to Geneva, the N.G.S. says "Rosemary is doing a splendid job." This appointment was only temporary as she was anxious to have experience in community and field work. In March she took over the Homework Club and other activities at Ofafa and then went on to supervise some of the village work. Meanwhile the N.G.S. was negotiating with the C.C.K. to find Rosemary some training overseas. By September, a scholarship had been obtained to Swansea University for a two year diploma course in social work.

Jean Ngoima, a member of one of the YM/YW groups in Kiambu decided to give up her career as a teacher to become Assistant Warden, Beecher House. It was not long before Edna realised that Jean was worthy of further training and she succeeded in obtaining a year's scholarship for her at Bath Domestic Science College. The N.G.S. notified World YWCA as funds were needed for her air passage and board and lodging. In June, $550 was received from Geneva, being a gift through Mrs. Cedergren of the Swedish Womens' Ecumenical Council. Jean began her training in September. At the end of the year, her examination results were so good that she was offered a further year's training in Institutional Management at Shrewsbury Domestic Science College. Jean and Rosemary, therefore, returned to Kenya together in 1966.

Esther Wairumu, one of the first graduates from the School, having had a term's experience as Assistant Matron/Housekeeper at a teacher training college, then almost a year as Assistant Warden Beecher House, had been a very successful Warden of Ofafa. It was felt that she too was worthy of some further training. The N.G.S. therefore approached the Ministry of Education, feeling that, if they would grant Esther a scholarship, it would prove that the YWCA School was recognised by the Kenya Government authorities. It took several visits and letters to persuade the authorities that a girl with only eight years formal schooling would benefit from further education in the U.K. Eventually Esther was given a Government scholarship for one year to Bath Domestic Science College to start with Jean in September.

Vera wrote to Janet Little, Head of International Department, British YWCA, giving the names of Rosemary, Jean, and Esther and details of their courses. Janet made contact on their arrival and kept in touch with them by post throughout their period in the U.K. During their vacations, they all enjoyed seeing something of the Association in Britain. They were entertained by Janet at National Headquarters and by various friends of Vera's in England and Scotland. Esther returned to Nairobi in September 1965 and joined the YWCA staff.

In January 1964 Mrs. Kiano called to see Vera to say that she felt that a Kenya born woman should be National President now that the country was independent and that she had asked Vice-President Mrs. Gecaga to act for her until the next meeting of the Executive. Mrs. Kiano was what is now termed "a black American".

It was Jemima Gecaga, therefore, who greeted Princess Sophia when she visited Kenya with her father, the Emperor Haile Selassi. The Princess was National President of the Ethiopian YWCA which had been recently founded.

The N.G.S. formally introduced Mrs. Margaret Mugu to the Executive at the January Meeting and it was agreed that she should start working in the National Office on 1st February. As the two hostels in Kirk Road were working so well together, thanks to the efforts of the late Miss Pole, it was decided that the post of Hostels Director was no longer necessary. In future each house would have its own warden.

Isabel Catto, who had recently retired as World President, visited East Africa, arriving in Kenya on 20th February for one month. It was too soon after Independence for her to be able to make any assessment of how the Association would be organised in the new Kenya. She met Margaret Kenyatta, daughter of His Excellency the President, and Emma Njonjo, Director of Home Economics and shortly to become Director of Women's Education in Kenya. Miss Njonjo told Miss Catto that she considered the YWCA School to be of a very high standard. Miss Catto also paid a visit to Mombasa.

Early in the year the first official National Council of Women of Kenya was founded and Margaret Kenyatta was elected President. A great deal of discussion took place regarding the Constitution of this new Council, some members recommending that individual membership should be made available, as in the Constitution of the British Council of Women. Margaret however, considered that this would cause confusion and was strongly in favour of the Council being an umbrella organisation to include all women's movements in Kenya. Being under some considerable pressure, she called at the YWCA to ask Vera's opinion. Vera wholeheartedly agreed that what was needed was a Council to which all women's organisations in Kenya could affiliate and that no individual membership should be permitted; this in fact is what ensued. Prior to the founding of the National Council, the YWCA was the only multi-racial organisation for women in Kenya.

Into the New Kenya — 1964

On the day of Margaret Kariuki's wedding, there was much excitement in the School; all the senior Trainees were driven to the Church. The bride was given away by her father, the Bishop of Fort Hall, and the Archbishop conducted the Service. As the bride and groom left the Church, the twelve Trainees formed a Guard of Honour. Doreen Boedeker, Edna Collins and Vera Harley, were all at the Service. So Margaret became Mrs. Waiyaki and soon she was doing voluntary work in Undunyu Village, assisting Mrs. Mary Martin of the Friends Service Council, teaching literacy and child care.

By March, the YWCA was fully staffed. Susan Thumbe, who had been Chairman of the University YWCA Group, having obtained her degree in Home Economics was taking over as Headmistress of the Vocational Training School and Warden of Beecher House. Mrs Boedeker, whose position had now been ratified, still with the loyal Mrs Venn as her assistant, was running International House splendidly, two graduates from the School working as Receptionist and Housekeeper. An extremely good African Cateress had been a appointed; she had recently qualified in Britain. It was now decided that a Night Warden should be employed to check on residents returning late at night. Such a post was last mentioned in 1947.

The Executive meeting on the 28th April, held in Windsor House Quiet Room, was a crucial one. Some of the African Committee Members considered that Margaret Mugo should be able to learn the National General Secretary's job in six months. Margaret was offered the post as from the National Council in July, but she refused to accept unless Vera Harley remained with her until February 1965, being a full calendar year. Feeling that her presence was an embarrassment, Vera offered to leave the meeting. The Chairman, Mrs. Gecaga, complied, saying that Mrs. Mugu should leave also. Many years later, Margaret and Vera laughed about the time they sat together on a rock in the garden enjoying the sunshine wondering what their fate was going to be. There must have been a lengthy debate, for it was some time before a servant was sent to recall them. It had been agreed, that at Council in July Margaret would become N.G.S. and Vera should be asked to stay on as Consultant for six months. In May, Mrs. Kiano asked Executive if she could become a Vice-President and relinquish her position as National President. This was agreed and Mrs. Gecaga was asked to act as National President until elections at Council.

A conference took place in Dar-es-Salaam in May and, for the first time, Mrs Mugo represented the Kenya Association. The theme was "The Church's responsibility in an Urban setting".

Over the past five years, almost fifty girls had graduated from the School and Edna thought it was time for a reunion. It was, of course, realised that only those living in or near Nairobi would be able to attend but over a dozen arrived, all of

Rickshaws to Jets

them in jobs, some married with their children — one of the little girls was called Vera! It was a very happy tea party.

Good Hostess Courses continued and in May a course for Police Wives was so well attended that some of the students had to be found beds in the Hostels, the Prefab accommodating only twelve. This was not easy as Beecher and International Houses were almost full, girls of all races living in both.

Fork Luncheons were still very popular and frequently ladies from the newly established Embassies attended, thus giving an international dimension which was very important.

The YWCA was invited to send a representative to Machakos where the Government of Israel had donated a college for Women's Community Development. The N. G. S had a previous commitment, so Edna Collins attended. The College was opened by His Excellency the President, Jomo Kenyatta, and Edna was fortunate enough to meet and talk with him. He was extremely interested to hear about the Vocational Training School and the Good Hostess courses.

Executive Committee felt that an Assistant General Secretary should be recruited to take responsibility for programme work and to act for the new N.G.S. in her absence. Mrs Nellie Njage was appointed. At the same meeting, Mrs Tameno reported that she had secured a plot of land in Ngong and a YWCA room had already been built. On 18th May, the N.G.S. was invited to the opening of this Centre which was to be a Day Nursery. The plot had been donated and a local builder had done the work free of charge. A second Day Nursery was to open in a nearby village within the next few months.

The Mombasa Branch had requested Geneva to send them a European General Secretary and in May Miss Kathleen Holthusen arrived, having had experience in New Zealand, Pakistan and Canada. After a few days in Nairobi, Vera went with her to the Coast to introduce her to Mombasa members and help her into the job.

The Manager of Barclays Bank, Dar-es-Salaam, happened to be an old family friend of Vera's and on several occasions he rang to book accommodation for girls coming to Nairobi for training. They were always found rooms in the Higher Income Hostel. All of them had graduated from high school with School Certificate and were being trained for the Bankers' Institute Examination. Barclays was the first of the Banks to offer African girls a career in banking and excellent opportunities were given for promotion.

In June, Edna Collins told Executive that she wished to return to C.M.S. work in September. She assured the Committee that Beecher House and the School were being run efficiently by Susan Thumbe who was well supported by three graduates from the School, working as Housekeeper, Receptionist and Cateress. Ofafa Hostel was rapidly filling up and Mrs. Olive Rogers had been appointed to take over as Warden when Esther left for U.K. The Day Nursery there, with its Training School, was going very well and Miss Minami, the volunteer from Japan,

Into the New Kenya — 1964

said that, as two of the Trainees were of exceptionally high standard, she would like to recommend them for scholarships in Japan. So the N.G.S. contacted the newly established Japanese embassy and they kindly arranged for the girls to have lessons in Japanese. The Ambassador's wife invited the N.G.S. and Edna Collins, together with the two fortunate students, for lunch at her house; she sensibly thought it important that these girls should experience some Japanese food and customs before leaving in July for their year's training at Houriku Gakuin College.

The National Council met on 4th July 1964 and the Archbishop opened the meeting with prayer. Mrs Gecaga was in the Chair and, during the course of the meeting, she was elected National President. The attendance was very good, all branches being represented. Elections were held which resulted in the number on Executive committee being brought up to 28; of these, 19 were non-European.

In her Report, the N.G.S. congratulated the Appeals and Publicity Committee for having raised K.shs 140,000 in the last five years. The two new Standing Committees, Finance and Personnel had been extremely helpful, Mrs Ann Ndegwa was Chairman of the latter. The YM/YW Committee had not proved to be successful. The YMCA, however, were funding a Women's Training Centre at Kiambu which was doing good work. The YWCA Education and Training Committee were taking a keen interest and giving every possible assistance. One of the graduates from the School was a paid member of staff there. The N.G.S. listed the guests who had been welcomed at Headquarters during the year:

Princess Sophia, National President YWCA Ethiopia
Mrs Mildred Marlie, YWCA South Africa
Miss Lettie Stuart, Sierra Leone and World YWCA staff
Miss Ishi-Bashi of Japan and World YWCA staff
Mrs Kent of the British YWCA
Miss Jean Ballard of New Zealand and a member of World Executive Committee.
Miss Leila Anderson, International Secretary YWCA U.S.A.

Being a very important Council meeting, the press was present, also television cameras, and the K.B.C. broadcast in the News that the Kenya YWCA had appointed an African National General Secretary, Mrs Margaret Mugo and went on to say that the previous N.G.S. was to return to England. They didn't say in six months time. On 6th July, Vera Harley became 'Consultant'.

In August, Nellie Njagi organised a Holiday Club for schoolchildren. They met every week day in the Conference Room. She also organised a very successful dance in International House lounge with a splendid Congolese band.

During August, Mr Tom Mboya was invited to give a lecture tour in Australia and his wife, Pamela, accompanied him. As before her marriage she had been a Hostel resident, and was now a member of Executive Committee, Vera wrote to YWCA Headquarters in Australia, giving details of the visit. When they returned to Kenya, Pamela told Vera that, whenever they arrived in a hotel, there were flowers to greet her from the local YWCA, always asking if they could meet her. As she was there to support her husband, she had little spare time, but on several occasions a short visit to the local YWCA. was arranged. At their last port of call, Melbourne, the usual bouquet having arrived, she decided that she must accept their invitation for lunch. She telephoned to thank them for the flowers and said she would be free that morning. By midday, the Melbourne Association had not only laid on a delicious lunch, but had mustered a large group of members to meet Pamela. It is occasions like this that emphasise the world family which is the YWCA.

A very kind letter was received from Gertrude Friedrich, National General Secretary of the German YWCA and a member of World Executive. She spoke of the continued interest of her Association in the Kenya YWCA and she concluded: "Kenya still remains a special task for me, to which part of my heart belongs." It will be remembered that it was due to the generosity of her Association that funds for Vera Harley's last tour were made available.

At the August Executive, Miss Grace John, now President, Mombasa, told the Committee that their Hostel was only half full and that the financial situation was very critical. This was partly because many Europeans had left the country and very few African or Asian girls at the coast required accommodation. She was more cheerful about the Club activities however, saying that the groups in Mombasa, Freretown, Buxton and Tudor, still under the guidance of Mrs Kitty Hall, were going well. She paid special tribute to Monica Murphy, their V.S.O., who would shortly be leaving after her year's service.

On 1st September, Edna Collins left the staff and rejoined C.M.S. She had been with the Association for five and half years and had done a remarkable job. Not only had she been responsible for starting Beecher House Hostel, but she had created the Vocational Training School which had produced the best results for the London Council of Domestic Studies examinations, in the whole of Kenya. After Mary Suthren's departure, she had taken responsibility for her work, training African girls to take over from her. She had set up Ofafa and started the Day Nursery and taken responsibility for it until the arrival of the trained volunteers from the U.S.A. and Japan. During Miss Pole's tragic illness, when the N.G.S. was still in U.K., she had somehow managed to keep everything going. Sincere gratitude was expressed to Edna and to the C.M.S. for seconding her to the Association.

The Meru branch invited Vera to visit them during the first week of October, so, together with Doreen Boedeker, she left on the Saturday morning. When she arrived, Vera visited the Methodist Mission, Meru Christians being predominately Methodist, and then called on the District Commissioner, before meeting with the YWCA group. She found them to be very enthusiastic and they asked her to meet

Into the New Kenya — 1964

them again the following morning (Sunday) before returning to Nairobi. As they drove back, Vera, wondering if she would ever be in that beautiful part of the world again, asked Thogo to stop at Nanyuki so that she could stand across the Equator whilst enjoying, perhaps for the last time, a beautiful view of Mount Kenya. Looking at the mountain, the second highest in Africa, being over 17,000 feet, she remembered what a Kikuyu friend had told her about the origin of the name, "Kirinyaga" in the tribal language, describing so imaginatively the black rock and white glacier as the wing of the male ostrich; translated it meant, "Ostrich up there!" The name of the country, is, of course, derived from this.

At the request of Executive, Vera left the following Tuesday for Mombasa as news from there was not good. She flew down on the "milk" plane at 4.00 a.m., there being no room on the train. On arriving, she found Kathleen Holthusen in a nervous condition and far from well, with Beatrice and Ada, the two ex-Trainees, and an excellent V.S.0., Ruth Cooper, ably holding the fort with good support from the committee. Vera's brief was to make a report on on-going work, to make a survey of accommodation needs and, together with the Honorary Auditor, make a report of the financial situation. After a week, Vera persuaded Kathleen Holthusen to take two weeks leave. The Hostel was empty except for an occasional transit guest and three V.S.O.s who were working with various agencies at the Coast. Both Ada and Beatrice's parents lived in Mombasa, so Vera decided to pay off the two remaining male domestic staff and, in order to comply with Union Rules, she officially closed the Hostel for three days, first making sure that the three V.S.O.s were safely housed. A night watchman was engaged. Kitty Hall and her husband, Commander John Hall, who lived opposite the Hostel, were of tremendous help and support, Vera and Ruth being given hospitality by them until the Hostel re-opened. Kitty was able to furnish Vera with all the information she needed for part of her brief. The educational groups were still going well, as were the local branches. The Hostel needed an experienced Warden who could manage domestic staff. As for accommodation needs, it was doubtful if there was a sufficient number of girls who could afford to live in the YWCA. if it continued to be run as a high income hostel. Kitty felt that, if something could be set up on the Beecher House model, it would be far more practical. After three days, Vera and Ruth, Ada and Beatrice and the three V.S.O.s moved back to the Hostel and Vera completed her Report. As soon as Kathleen Holthusen returned, Vera was recalled to Nairobi by the National President.

During November, Dr Alice Arnold of World YWCA visited Kenya, She spent a few days in Nairobi before going to Mombasa for a long weekend.

The Christmas market was held on 28th November at International House and raised £830.

Then came Christmas, with the now well established midday dinner in International House for any resident from any Hostel who wished to join in and bring their friends. This year several of the domestic staff had their wives and children living in the compound. Doreen found that there were 14 children and, after Christmas Dinner, she and Vera met them all in Beecher House Garden and gave each child a present.

On 26th December, Margaret Mugo flew to Nigeria to represent the Association at a W.C.C. Conference for women.

1965. Training Centre for Mombasa

During January, the School examination results arrived from London. They were excellent, all the students having passed the London Council of Domestic Studies examination in every subject. By now, about 60 girls had qualified from the YWCA School and all were holding down jobs, several with the Association, working in Hostels or organising educational programmes in villages. Some were working in community centres in Nairobi, others for the Department of Education as matrons or caterers in boarding schools and colleges and one was employed as an unqualified teacher in an Intermediate school. Two were House Mothers in Dr Barnardo's Home in Nairobi; one was working with the Church Army. Two were working at the YM/YW centre in Kiambu, another was on the staff of the women's prison. Two were working for Maendeleo ya Wanawaki. Another was Housekeeper at the Israeli Community Development college. One was an instructress for Singer Sewing Machines, two were working in Nairobi offices and one was a cookery demonstrator for the E.A.P.&L. This remarkably varied list of occupations demonstrated how beneficial the comprehensive syllabus had proved to be.

The 1965 Convention was held on 10th 11th and 12th January at the Mombasa Hostel, the first time it had taken place outside Nairobi. As there were now no residents, the Hostel made an excellent residential conference centre. The staff from HQ were Vera Harley and Nellie Njage. They arrived to find Kathleen Holthusen with severe back trouble and unable to move. What was more the cook had left! However, with the help of Ada and Beatrice, and the excellent V.S.O. Ruth Cooper, Vera was able to organise the food. Unlike 1964, the Convention was very well attended, delegates having travelled long distances from all parts of Kenya. After the first day, Kathleen Holthusen, although unwell, was able to join the Conference.

The N. G. S opened the Convention, telling the delegates that this would be her last opportunity of meeting with them all. She asked them to think back to the time when they first joined the Association and suggested they tried to remember why they had joined. As everyone knew, there were now several organisations for women and girls in Kenya, but none of the others was multi-racial, ecumenically Christian, but with membership open to women and girls of all creeds. It was therefore an all embracing Movement. She reminded Full Members that they had dedicated themselves to the service of others and said that there could be no limit

Into the New Kenya — 1965

Bathing party at the end of the 1965 Annual Convention in Mombasa

to the quality of that service. She then quoted something that Jean Begg had said to her when congratulating her on a piece of work she had carried out in Egypt in 1944. "Yes dear," J. B. had said to Vera, "It's very good, but remember, because we have that "C" in our name, it can never be good enough." This, she said, was a tremendous challenge. Other organisations carried out programmes similar to that of the YWCA and it was up to the Full Members to ensure that the Association's standards were as high as or even higher than any other. There must be no envy or jealousy, but co-operation and loyalty. Reminding them of the YWCA motto, she urged them to live by it. She told them that there was a saying that the quality of a nation may be measured by the quality of its women. In conclusion, she said "I leave this thought with you."

Patron Mrs Betty Stratton, whose name appears in this history as Mrs Galton-Fenzi as far back as the 1930s and later as Mrs Montgomery, once the very active President of Nairobi Branch, was now a widow for the third time and living just outside Mombasa in a house on the seashore. On the last afternoon, she invited everyone to go for tea and a swim. Knowing of this before leaving Nairobi, Vera had borrowed as many swimsuits as she could lay hands on as she knew that most members did not possess such garments — indeed most of them had never seen the sea before. It was a wonderful adventure and everyone greatly enjoyed the Patron's hospitality. Mrs Stratton, now an old lady, was delighted. It was a very fulfilling experience for her having served the Association for so many years, through all its vicissitudes, and worked so hard to include African women and girls in the YWCA. She told Vera that she was thrilled to see such progress and to meet so many young and enthusiastic African members. Maggie Gona, a founder member of the Mombasa Branch, remembers Vera saying to her at the end of the

Margaret Mugo with her mother outside her parents' house with moonflowers

Convention "Maggie, this is your country and your YWCA so now it's up to you." Twenty four years later, Maggie was elected National Chairman.

During Vera's last few weeks in Kenya, one of the African members who was Chairman of a Standing Committee, said she found it difficult to think of prayers with which to start meetings. She was a Presbyterian, so Vera suggested she should extemporise. This, she said, she could not do and she asked Vera to leave her some suitable prayers. Time was short, so turning to her Anglican Book of Common Prayer (Edward VI version), Vera selected ten Collects and had them typed out for her.

On 30th January, a farewell tea party was given for Vera and she was presented with a cheque and a picture of Mount Kenya and was offered the use of her flat rent free until the beginning of March.

Vera had been to Margaret Mugo's home on several occasions and met her husband and children, but she had never met her parents. Margaret was determined to put this right before Vera left Kenya, so, one afternoon, they drove to the village where Margaret had lived before her marriage. Many years later, the thing that Vera remembered most clearly, was the beautiful moon-flower trees blooming in front of the house. Margaret's father spoke English and Vera was welcomed most graciously by her parents and shown the family Bible. After tea, Margaret said that she wanted to walk down to the river so that Vera could see the place from which, as a girl, she had collected the family water supply every morning and evening. This, and gathering firewood, were the tasks always allocated to daughters. Fortunately, by then, there was a pump in the parents' garden. On the way back to the car, they met Margaret's grandmother, 'Shushu' in Kikuyu. Vera was introduced and warmly greeted. The old lady was dressed in traditional Kikuyu costume, one shoulder bare, knee-length skirt, bare feet and adorned with earrings and necklaces. Whilst driving back to Nairobi, Margaret explained that

Into the New Kenya — 1965

Shushu had been too old to benefit from the education which missionaries had brought to the country. She was, therefore, not Christian and only when Kikuyus were baptised did they wear European clothes. The events of the afternoon reminded Vera of something Driver Thogo had told her some years previously. His family had consisted of two girls, and it was ten years before his wife bore him a son. By the time the boy was nine and old enough to give a helping hand, the daughters had left home, so his father told him that he must help his mother, collecting firewood and water. The boy was very upset, saying that the other boys laughed at him for doing "girls' work." Thogo then had a bright idea; he asked the village fundi to make a small wheelbarrow and to paint it bright red. This he gave his son for Christmas. Before long, the boy was collecting the family wood and water, proudly using his wheelbarrow, much to the envy of his peers.

During February, Vera was able to visit all the YWCA and YM/YW groups within 30 miles or so of Nairobi to say goodbye. It was when she was with a large gathering of YM/YW members in the Kiambu District that the local African clergyman, who was chairing the function, said that they would all miss "Makena." Vera knew that the Kikuyu people were famous for giving nicknames which they usually kept secret. As everyone laughed, she realised that this was the name by which she was known. On the way back to Nairobi, she asked driver Thogo what it meant. He laughed and she was relieved to be told that the translation was "The Happy One."

After despatching her heavy baggage to go by sea, Vera spent two months travelling in South and Central Africa. She returned to Nairobi and stayed with Lady Harragin before flying home. One lunchtime, Margaret Mugo telephoned, saying that Executive had met that morning and that she and two committee members would be calling to see Vera that afternoon. Lady Harragin had gone for her siesta before they arrived. The purpose of their visit was to ask Vera to cancel her flight home and stay for a year as Adviser in Mombasa. Pleased as Vera was to be asked, she explained that her family were now expecting her and her luggage had gone, so she would have to decline their offer. Soon after her return to England, Vera was very surprised to meet Mrs. Kiano, who was travelling on the same train to London. Ernestine was amazed and delighted, as her husband, who was then Minister of Trade and Industry, had been offered £10,000 by the Van Leer Foundation of the Netherlands to be given to a women's organisation in Kenya. The Foundation, however, had specified that the whole sum must be used for one project. Dr Kiano, knowing of his wife's interest, had offered this to the YWCA, but a definite reply was required very soon. Before leaving Nairobi, Mrs Kiano had taken the matter to the new National General Secretary, but there had been no time to consider a project. Vera suggested that the Likoni Hotel, which she remembered was for sale, should be purchased as an educational base for the Mombasa Branch. The consequence was that this was accepted by the

Margaret Mugo, N.G.S. YWCA Kenya, visits the Mombasa Hostel

Foundation and the Hotel was acquired towards the end of the year to become an excellent secretarial school for some years, and later a residential training and conference centre.

Vera visited Bath to see Jean and Esther and they, as did Rosemary Kairu, stayed with her in London. Jean, after her two years' training, returned to Nairobi and worked with Mrs Boedeker at International House, taking responsibility for the training of hostel staff. She also visited the Hostel in Kampala at the request of Uganda YWCA. On Doreen's retirement in 1968, Jean became Hostels Director and Adviser to all YWCA Hostels in Kenya. When Rosemary returned, she became National Field and Extension Officer. After her marriage, she was voted on to Executive and, a few years later, became National Chairman. When this news reached Mary and Vera, they remembered that Rosemary had been the first Chairman of the African Girls' High School Y-teens; this was real YWCA.

So ends the story of the first 53 years of the Kenya YWCA, years of tremendous change and development in every sphere. Sincere gratitude must be expressed to all the loyal, hard working volunteers who, over the years, served the Association both in Nairobi and Mombasa, not forgetting the many men who gave their expertise in law, finance, insurance and building. Special mention must be made of the Right Reverend William George Peel, the first Bishop of Mombasa, who gave the Association in its early years, tremendous encouragement and support, and even lent his house to be the first Hostel and of the first Archbishop of East Africa, the Most Reverend Leonard Beecher, who gave so much of his time and thought and so tactfully and skilfully guided the Association into becoming a multi-racial movement worthy of affiliation to World YWCA.

Thirty Years On

The Association has developed enormously and now has six Local Associations and a total membership of 12,000.

At the 1975 World Council in Vancouver, Kenya became fully affiliated under Category A. Margaret Mugo served as National General Secretary for 17 years, was elected to World Executive Committee and subsequently became a World Vice-President. After her retirement, she was elected National Chairman of the Kenya Association, serving for four years, Sadly she died in 1993.

Good, inexpensive accommodation is still an important part of the Association's work. The Nairobi Hostels are full and a third floor was added to Beecher House in 1969. Thirty two (32) self contained flats were built on the tennis courts in 1976. Ofafa is now Nairobi Branch Headquarters, offering accommodation for 92 girls and a day nursery for 64 children.

The Mombasa Association is very active, the Hostel filling an important need. The "Likoni Hotel" is now the Association's Training and Conference Centre. Hostels have been built in Kisumu and Meru, both branches have an active membership.

Whilst continuing with a programme of Adult Literacy, Health Education, Leadership Training and Community Service, associations around the country have developed a wide variety of important activities, such as Agro-forestry, Mango Marketing, Poultry Keeping, Bakeries and the installation of running water.

The Association has placed great emphasis on youth and 25 per cent of the National Board are women under the age of thirty.

In 1987, the Association celebrated its 75th Anniversary. Mrs Louisa Owiti who, for 15 years was General Secretary, Mombasa, became National General Secretary in 1986.

There is little doubt that the ladies who first met on St Valentine's day in 1912 would have been very proud.

Presidents/National Chairman Since 1965

1964 Mrs. Jemima Gecaga
1968 Mrs. Perpetua Kaigwa
1969 Mrs. Ann W. Ndegwa
1974 Mrs. Mary Omolo
1978 Mrs. Wanjiku Chiuri — née Rosemary Kairu
1981 Mrs. Margaret Mugo
1985 Dr. Pamela Kola
1989 Mrs. Maggie Gona
1993 Mrs. Mary Owuor

In 1972 Government decreed that the title "President" was to be reserved exclusively for the President of the Republic of Kenya thus from 1974 the YWCA senior office-bearer has been referred to as National "Chairman".

Bibliography

Capon, Rev M.G.	Towards Unity in Kenya
Duguid, Julian	The Blue Triangle
Committee of the Church of the Province of Kenya	Rabau to Mumias
Gatabaki, Njehu	The City of Nairobi
Likimani, Mathoni	Women of Kenya
Murray, Jocelyn	Proclaim the Good News
Rice, Anna V	A History of the World's Young Women's Christian Association
Rodwell, Edward	The Mombasa Club
Smart, James	Nairobi, a Jubilee History

Glossary

Ayah	Indian/African child's nurse
Debi	Four gallon kerosene tine. When empty used for domestic purposes
Dhow	Arab sailing boat/ship
Fundi	Indian/African workman, usually a specialist in some craft. An expert in making things and making things work
Gharry	Horse-drawn carriage or cart
Giriama	A coastal tribe in Kenya
Khanzu	White, full-length shirt worn by Arabs and some African house servants — Swahili
Makuti	Plaited branch of coconut palm used in building — Swahili
Murram	Crushed red rock used for surfacing roads
Rickshaw	Two-wheeled passenger vehicle drawn by a man
Shamba	Garden/Farm — small cultivated field. Arab/African — Swahili
Uhuru	Freedom
Wanawaki na Harambee	Women pulling together — Swahili

Re-named roads in Nairobi

Government Road	Moi Avenue
6th Avenue – Delamere Avenue	Kenyatta Avenue
Kirk Road	Nyerere Road
Jackson Road	Muindi Road
Protectorate Road	Mamlaka Road
Sadler Street	Koinange Street
Whitehouse Road	Haile Selassi Avenue
Market Street	Muindi Mbuigu Street
Eliot Street	Biashara Street
Portal Road	Banda Road